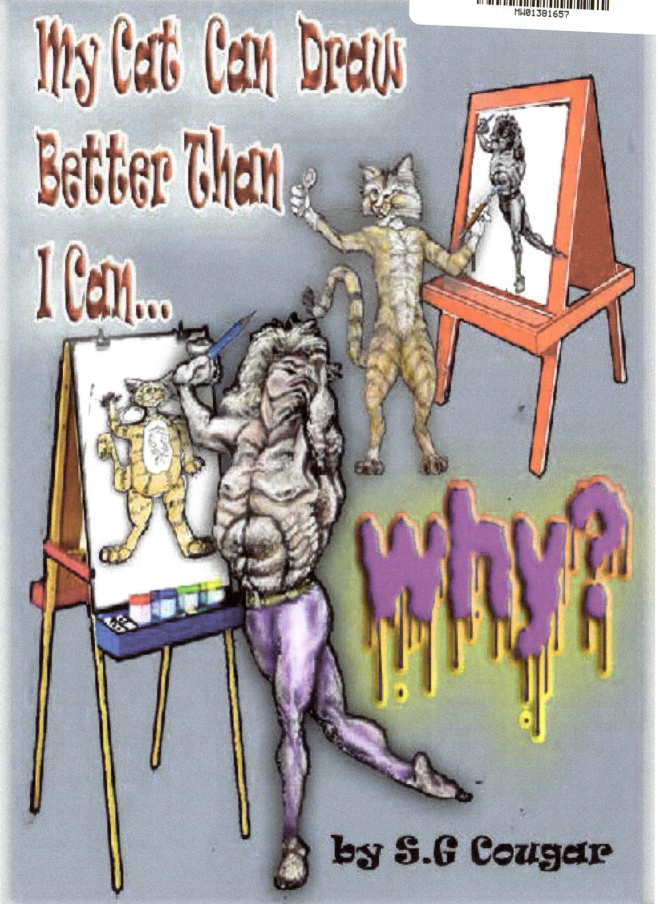

A QUICKIE BIO.
MY CAREER AS AN ARTIST & writer

Currently I have a studio called "CARTOON COUGAR STUDIO" and I am a graphic designer, cartoonist, illustrator, and art teacher.

Throughout the years, I have done many logos, animal and human portraits, graphic designs, from animal feed stores, beauty shops, real estate companies, animal and caricatures of clients at fair grounds, street fun events, and in my own shop

I have been published by Leatherneck magazine, ARC magazine, and Clark College newspaper.

I am also illustrating and helping to write a small musical book for a company called *"Whomp'n Pawz Productions LLC"* which I have helped start that helps kids get into the world of music. Starring a blue, magical harmonica playing cat called Bluzkat. This is still an ongoing mission.

I opened and ran my own Art School called, **GRAPHIC CAT SCHOOL OF ILLUSTRATION AND CARTOONING** for 12 years which included: teaching realistic art, cartooning, comic book, graphic book illustration, teaching 3-d clay anatomy, graphic art, fine art, tole painting, realistic/cartooning human and animal portrait drawing, creative advertising, and marketing techniques.

I did POP displaying shrink wrapping, directing art projects for students/clients. buying,/selling art materials, consulting with customers on printing, layout, and Illustrative techniques. Script writing. Hiring specialty teachers and teaching interested students how to become successful art teachers.

I have also taught in various high schools, grade schools, schools for the challenged, and at Tualatin Community Center for over 2 years, which I taught students of all ages air brush, cartooning, and illustration.

I have and still teaching students on line how to illustrate realistically and cartoon spot and strip cartoons where several of my students have gone on to successful art careers, and getting scholarships for their portfolio work.

Currently I have just started an art class for people in my church which promises to grow.

I have alwayls loved wood and tooling in leather. and am learning how to woodcarve, do relief work and woodburn. I have spent a summer selling my wooden projects.

MY CAREER AS A WRITER

After 15 years of security work as a Correctional Officer, I finally have finished my art book, "My Cat Can Draw Better Than I Can…WHY?" which is an accumulation of all my special drawing techniques I've been teaching my students .

My interests lay into historical fiction, and sci-fi .Now, I want to incorporate now on the worldly events that have been prophetically foretold by Jesus,Prophets and Apostles in Bible. I am currently working on a prophetic historical novel with a sci-fi bend to it called: "Time Of Sorrows."

I am sporadically writing and illustrating my own children's books. one of my current projects is a series of 4 small musical books illustrated and written by me to help musically challenged people that love music but, have no idea what a note is and how they work.

I have had a short history of writing comic book scripts for several clients.

I also have been a ghost writer for over 5 years.

When I had the **GRAPHIC CAT** I had taught students, hopeful writers and comic book script writers how organize their thoughts, plots, character development, helped them navagate through the dizzing world of publishing, and teaching them how to find editors, and agents.

AWARDS: I received the Edda McCormick scholarship for my art work in Clark College, and in 2005 was awarded first place for outstanding cartooning for C.O.W. (CARTOONIST OF Washington).

I am a member of the National Association of Professional women, which profiles the country's most accomplished PROFESSIONAL WOMEN throughout the nation.

DEDICATION

This book is dedicated to all my present and past students That has taught me how to draw, teach me to teach and what to teach.

Without their help, I could not have written this book.

I also dedicate this book to all the people along my life's path that has believed, encouraged, and has and had pushed me to finish this book and continue on with my cartooning, when I felt that nothing was going right.

THERE ARE A FEW SPECIAL PEOPLE THAT I WANT TO ESPECIALLY THANK

Jesus Christ, It is He that has given me the ability to get this book done. Without His gift of giving me the teaching ability and the artistic ability to get my points across this book never would have come into existence

Rochelle Teeny, who has been a brilliant friend for over 25 years, a former student, and now is helping me in editing this book. Her love and encouragement has been an inspiration for me all these years!.

Jamie Herbert, for her close friendship over 15 years and opening up her heart, mind, and continuing belief that I could create Bluzkat and Gang to help promote her musical dreams for kids with *"Pawz For Music."* Without her and encouragement and belief, my cartooning career would have died.

Larry Roth , He is a fantastically funny gag writer who has been an exceptional cartooning student that has also taught me to improve on my cartooning thru teaching him. I am eternally grateful to him for over his 15 year dedication as an art student and a superb friend.

Speedy Zawistowski,   He is an extremely funny gag writer who helped me publish my cartooning for the first time. He opened up the 'tooning door and gave me my first real look at being published. He has been my wonderful friend for over 25 years.

THANK YOU ALL!

CONTENTS

BOOK ONE - RULES

CHAPTER ONE	"WHAT'S WRONG WITH THIS PICTURE?"
CHAPTER TWO	RULES
CHAPTER THREE	LEARNING THE RULES
CHAPTER FOUR	'EL-FLATO'
CHAPTER FIVE	THE MAGICAL ILLUSION OF PERSPECTIVE
CHAPTER SIX	UNDERSTANDING VANISHING POINTS
CHAPTER SEVEN	CAMERA VIEW
CHAPTER EIGHT	HORIZON LINE

BOOK TWO - THEORIES

CHAPTER NINE	INTRODUCTION
CHAPTER TEN -	THE PHYSICS OF LUMPY AND BUMPY
CHAPTER ELEVEN	YOU ARE NOW A MICROBE
CHAPTER TWELVE	THE COFFEE CUP THEORY
CHAPTER THIRTEEN	THE SMILE AND FROWN THEORY
CHAPTER FOURTEEN	THE PROTRACTOR SPECULATION THEORY
CHAPTER FIFTEEN	THE HAPPY 'Y' & TIRED 'T' THEORY
CHAPTER SIXTEEN	THE COIN THEORY
CHAPTER SEVENTEEN	THE GLASS GHOST THEORY
CHAPTER EIGHTEEN	THE SPIDER WEB THEORY
CHAPTER NINETEEN	THE BUTTERFLY MORPHING THEORY
CHAPTER TWENTY	THE BUCKING BRONCO THEORY
CHAPTER TWENTY ONE	'WHY ARE YOU LOOKING AT YOUR THUMB?" THEORY
CHAPTER TWENTY TWO	SUMMARY

"My Cat Can Draw Better Than I Can! ...WHY?"

A NEW WAY OF LOOKING HOW TO DRAW

S.G. COUGAR

BOOK ONE
RULES
CHAPTER ONE
"WHAT'S WRONG WITH THIS PICTURE?"

How do I take this picture seen on the left…and not make look like this picture on the right?"

"How do I make what I see look real or look like the picture I am copying?"

" How do I draw it the way I see it?"

"Why do all my objects such as tables, and chairs, cups and saucers, look like they are going up in the air?"

"Why do all my pictures look flat and out of proportion when I first draw my piece."

"Why does my realistic picture look like a cartoon?"

"*What* am I missing in my shading? I can't seem to get it to look 'touchable and believable!

" Why does my colored piece look so unnatural and flat?"
In one simple word I will sum up what issues all artists face….

PERSPECTIVE

(Ok…there will be more art "WORDS" that will further your understanding in the process of art, and I will get to those, but basically, perspective is the cornerstone of any understanding of getting your masterpiece to look real, and believable because that word encompasses a whole passel of art techniques that you must know in order to master this skill.)

Volumes have been written on this subject, and yet this word strikes **fear** in most artists!

Right away that word has put a block of negativity in the minds of a lot of artists!
"Perspective," is like telling the artist that they need to know Einstein's theory of Relativity!

I was in the same boat! I wanted to be an aspiring cartoonist, and I thought, "Oh, I don't need to know perspective! A cartoonist can get away with murder and I can draw well enough to get the point across. What I draw comes out ok, and as a cartoo
nist it doesn't really matter how my drawing looks because cartooning has many different styles.
So what if my drawing is off a bit, I still can fudge
my way into the magazines especially if I have a
wonderful gag line!"

I remember one of my first attempts of trying to do a
'cartoon' for a friend of mine who was a fireman at the time…so, at the ripe old age of 15
I drew this mess (I lost the original,
but I will NEVER forget what my feeble attempts of trying to be
funny looked like…) I thought at the time
that it was pretty good. I know now that the cat could have
drawn better in his litter box!

But, through time and lots of drawings, I was starting to 'get' it, ,
but, mostly because I was copying what I saw,but still not really
understanding what I was drawing!

I wasn't paying any attention to the PHYSICS of this shape.
So I shaded it like a flat 2 dimensional coloring book.
I did not take into consideration of how the object was…..

Constructed.
And because of this, my drawings still looked flat and
undeveloped.

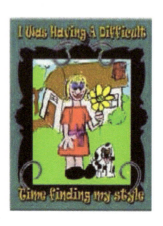

I still couldn't make such mundane things like roads, plates or tables look flat enough to place objects on it, or worse yet…I couldn't figure out how the surface of an object was affected by where I was looking…

IE if a picture of a table made me feel as I was looking down on it (or birds-eye view) and I tried to draw it, the stupid thing would always look like it was going straight up in the air!

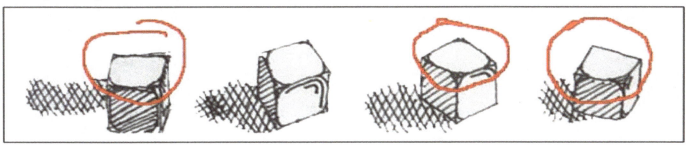

And the surface of the table always looked the same no matter if I was above it, looking straight at it, or a bit below it, I was frustrated and was beginning to view the drawing pad as an enemy!

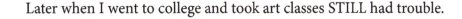

Later when I went to college and took art classes STILL had trouble.

My art teacher knew how to draw and make things look real on paper, but their advice didn't do me a bit of good because they couldn't explain was HOW they did it.

They just told the class…"keep on sketching and eventually you will get it!"

This advice to me that was like the example of putting a million monkeys in a room with typewriters and maybe in 150 years they MIGHT be able to type out the first page of the Bible.

I eventually started to "GET IT," on understanding the mechanics of perspective.

I started to see that things get smaller as they go back, and horizon line stuff, and the 1,2,3, point system. But…too mechanical, with no heart, and I knew it.

I still was missing some basic understanding with the building blocks of perspective as you can see with this picture on the right. The horses head is way too small for his body. (I was still struggling with anatomy.)

It finally dawned on me that there HAD to be a better way of getting this necessary "evil' across to them in a way that they would be fun for them and they would never forget these important rules.

I still had to use the verbiage and showing the students the correct steps but there was still one key element I was missing until I saw the students sketch book and the light bulb went on.

It was a student's picture of a dog that I was showing on how to get the nose right when I happened to wave my hand over the nose as if the nose was a 'bridge' and

BAM! There was the answer... **MOVEMENT!**

I actually SAW how I could get this concept across to the students on **HOW** the nose of this dog was a 3-dimensional block, combined with curvilinear properties to make the animal become real and understandable.

Putting these two 'discoveries' to work, I showed my students how to become a **SUPER DUPER, "MICRO-BUG,"** and made them imagine that they were traveling upon the lumpy and bumpy surface of the object they were drawing, ...I and my students were in art heaven!

This was the beginning of how I got my students to start putting 'gravy' upon the dry bones of perspective.

Unfortunately perspective is NOT a simple subject, and it is a technique that the artist is always going to be constantly tested when they draw their masterpieces.

But with beginning knowledge of movement and understanding of the **physics** of the subject I knew that this would be the key to be able to draw anything with confidence.

Now, of course, masters have known about this for centuries, and I am sure that there are millions of artists out there that also know this.

Unfortunately in all the years of art school, and college there wasn't ONE teacher could relay this visual concept to their students.

So, I would like to now try and get these many rules across to you in a way that you can visualize and understand the ancient, confusing maze of rules and theories that will make you an artist.

I will start the first section of this book out with:

SO, let's get started… The first thing you need to be introduced to is the rules.

If you don't know them, it is like a 'greenhorn' rider trying to get his horse going in a lush field of grass! The horse is going to stop and eat no matter what you do to him if you don't know the rules on how to get him going.

Art is no different than learning math, or putting a car together.

All subjects have 'pieces, and there's a name to these pieces.

One has to be introduced to the pieces and learn their names.

Then learn what they do and how these concepts apply to their art work.

You cannot put a car together until you understand what a tie rod is and does, or a carburetor, or a piston.

Art is no different

Just for kicks, here are some words and the theories behind them that you will be knowing and using all the time…

SOME COMMON ART WORDS WHICH YOU NEED TO LEARN FOR THEY ARE THE SKELETAL OR FRAME WORK IN WHICH TO START YOUR ART JOURNEY. THESE WORDS ARE THE RULES!

(these words are just the tip of the iceberg, but they are enough for you to get started. They are used constantly by experienced artists and is necessary for you to be properly educated in this field. Without the knowledge of these words you will become hopelessly lost.)

DIMENSION, PERSPECTIVE, EYE LEVEL, BIRDS EYE, WORMS EYE, HORIZON LINE, CAMERA VIEW, WEIGHT, MASS, 1 POINT, 2 POINT, 3 POINT.

THEORIES
These will put THE 'FLESH' ON THE ART SKELETAL 'RULES.'
(these theories are MY made up titles to help you understand HOW to get your drawing to look correct and WHY these theories are so necessary to apply to your drawings.)

"HAPPY Y" AND 'TIRED T", THE TABLE EDGE THEORY, "THE 'FROWN, AND SMILE" THEORY, THE "COFFEE CUP" THEORY THE 'COIN' THEORY, "THE GHOST THEORY."

And much more.

CHAPTER TWO
THIS BOOK IS IN TWO PARTS.
1. BASIC RULES
2. THEORIES

These two parts will be the 'skeleton' and the 'flesh' of drawing well.
These rules have been in existence since "Adam was a cowboy in knickerbockers" and there are hundreds of artists out there that have their own theory of HOW to draw well.
I am no different. But, as a teacher of thirty plus years, I have honed these rules down to two basic categories which I hope will cut to the chase and simplify these 'mysterious' steps in order to draw well.

THE FIRST PART OF THIS BOOK IS:

THE RULES

They are what you *MUST* know, and understand in order to draw with accuracy. Unfortunately *"THE RULES"* are usually the burr under the saddle blanket which causes a lot of trouble for beginners if they are not explained right. So, you need to understand these before you successfully can go onto the **"THEORIES"** section of book two.

"THE THEORIES" are the 'FILLERS'- IN' OR THE 'ROUNDERS- OUT' OF THE "RULES."
The theories are what will make your drawing come alive and exciting. They will be the "finishing touches" that you will need to complete your art education.

"THE BASIC RULES
THE MAGICAL ILLUSION OF PERSPECTIVE
PHYSICS
'EL-FLAT-O'

THE MAGIC OF FOUR
1. DIMENSION
1 dimension
2 dimension
3 dimension

2. VANISHING POINTS
1 point
2 point
3 point

3. EYE LEVEL (OR "CAMERA VIEW")
Eye level
Bird's eye
Worms eye

4. HORIZON LINE
Which I call:
"Home Base "for all vanishing points

SECOND SECTION OF THIS BOOK WILL CONSIST OF 12 THEORIES

1. **THE PHYSICS OF LUMPY AND BUMPY-** theory. Artistically understanding the PHYSICS of a living object which will start you on the road to understand how to make your picture come alive

2. **YOU ARE NOW A MICROBE TRAVELING OVER 'LUMPY AND BUMPY " SURFACE** theory- lessons of how to mentally feel the surface of the object you are drawing, which helps you render a more dynamic picture.

3. **"THE COFFEE CUP THEORY AND HOW NOT TO LOOK LIKE A GREEN HORN WHEN DRAWING THE OVAL"** theory. Mentally seeing and understanding the physics in something round or oval and applying it to foreshortening.

4 THE *"SMILE & FROWN "* theory. This is a 'shortcut' on how to look at the edge of something round or oval from a picture, and tell what depth the camera view is, either from a birds eye or worms eye view. This is an extension of the 'Coffee Cup' theory.

5. *"THE HAPPY "Y" & TIRED "T"* theory. This is a short cut on finding an angle on a box or rectangle from a PICTURE. Helping you tell if the camera is looking at the object as a birds eye or worms eye view.

6. *" THE PROTRACTOR SPECULATION"* theory -This is a shortcut to look at the corner angles of a box or rectangle and using an imaginary and real protractor to get the correct corner degree of these shapes.

7. *"THE GLASS GHOST"* theory - Lessons in seeing through the object in order to draw everything in proportion, especially if the object is at a three quarter view.

8. *"THE COIN."* Theory- lessons for finding the middle line on anything, which helps you find proper perspective in a turned object.

9. *"THE BUCKING BRONCO "* theory- the study of movement in your drawings.

10. *"THE SPIDER-WEB "* theory…Understanding how to look for negative shapes within the positive shapes to achieve accuracy when coping a picture.

11. *"THE BUTTERFLY MORPHING"* theory-Taking a stick drawing adding 2-d squares, rectangles, circles and triangles onto it, then "morphing' these 2-d shapes into 3-d blocks, pyramids, spheres, & cylinders. Then 'playing' dot to dot' and connecting all of these with the right curvatures in order to complete your figures or objects.

12. *""WHY ARE YOU LOOKING AT YOUR THUMB?"* theory- lessons in sighting objects by eye and using your thumb or pencil for drawing accurate pictorial measurements.

CHAPTER 3
THE FIRST HURDLE:
LEARNING THESE RULES

IN THE BEGINNING, there are words…and the words shall lead you to understanding, and understanding will lead you to doing, and doing will lead you to doing well, and doing well will lead you to feeling successful, and success will lead you to learn more words.

But, these words must be put in such a way where the student won't be bogged down, or lose heart, and give up.

When I have taken a look at art books, I am amazed at the complicated way or even the jumbled way the ideas of "how to" are thrown at the beginning artist.

What may be simple to the author is usually too much for the student.

I have always believed that being educated in the field of your choosing is very important and that you are not being duped into the 'KING'S NEW CLOTHES,' theory where you try and fake your knowledge in order to look smart. Unfortunately in this field you cannot fake your way through it. You either know it or you don't.

So, it has been always my goal for my students to achieve what I like to call the "Michelangelo degree" of art.

I want them to be able to go out in this highly competitive world and be able to knock 'em dead with true knowledge of any field of art they choose.

Be it, comic book, animation, illustration, painting, or children's book illustration because the groundwork will be built on "Old Masters" foundation of realistic art.

There is so much opportunity out there that the "world is your oyster." But you need to have that one bedge of solid artistic knowledge to beat out the competition.

Everyone learns in their own way, their own pace, and their own time. Some are visual learners, some are readers and learn by books… others have to be shown and have someone by their side.

I would like to hit on as many aspects of the reader's learning abilities as possible. I will present the tricks of the trade in a way that I haven't seen being explained before.

When you learn something, it is important to learn things in sequence in order to remember WHY, HOW, WHO, WHAT, AND WHERE.

I don't ask the students…"WHAT IS art?" because that is not the problem. The problem is trying to help the struggling students' piece together WHY their pictures look so flat.

So, my first two questions are:

"WHAT WILL KEEP YOU DRAWING WITH PASSION FOR THE REST OF YOUR LIFE?"

And "HOW CAN I HELP IN MAKING THIS HAPPEN?"

I have found if you don't get the main basis of art explained correctly (with lots of visuals and fun examples and **SUCCESSFUL ARTISTIC PROJECTS**) that the student usually loses heart and their desire is killed.

I have always used **MANY** scenario examples to help students visualize what I am trying to say. One of my favorite examples is relating art to building a house.

The steps are:
1. Concrete floor- **FOUNDATION-**
2. Framework - **'SUB WORDS'**
3. Dry walls - **RULES**
4. Finishing the house- **THEORIES**

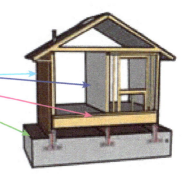

Unfortunately, there are many MORE steps to learning an putting in practice the principals of art just as there are a lot of steps in order to complete a beautiful house.
And **REMEMBERING EACH STEP** is the challenge!

1. You are *INTRODUCED* to the art vocabulary words.
(This is like speaking a foreign language to most students!)

2. Then they have to get *USE* to them
(you now have to say these words and repeat them in your brain, even if you don't know yet what they mean.)

3. Then you need to know what each word *MEANS.*
(this is where a teacher or book comes in to explain in words what they mean

4. Then you put what these words mean in by: *DRAWING.*

This process is very similar to being introduced to fifty strangers.

1. You are told their names, which will be impossible for the average person to remember.
2. But, as time goes by you start to associate the names with their faces.
3 Time and association has now imprinted each person's personality in your brain, and you are starting to be able to recognize who's who, by what they do.
4. Then with **CONSTANT REPETITION** seeing these people, saying their names and seeing their personalities you will eventually be able to remember them by sight and put their characterizations to their faces.

But, remember, Rome wasn't built in a day, so just take your time, and practice each step at your leisure…in fact one of my major rules to art is you do your best when you are mentally ready for it, and WANT to learn!

Never force yourself, for that is a quick way of feeling defeated, and yes, even bored with the subject.

Also, YOU need to know that every artist on this planet…yes, even the Masters had to struggle with learning this craft SO…

CHAPTER FOUR
The First "SLAP IN THE FACE"

Do you know that music and art both have many things in common?

When a music student first puts their fingers on a set of piano keys or blows through a wind instrument, their first notes usually are flat, wrong, and just a bunch of screeching, annoying noises.

The beginning works of learning students work is no different.

Their first attempt of putting pencil to paper is usually…

SO, WHY IS THIS?

THIS IS THE FIRST IMPORTANT QUESTION THAT IS ASKED. BUT, IT IS NOT A SIMPLE QUESTION TO ANSWER.

There is not "JUST ONE ANSWER" to this question.
There are a series of steps that one has to take in order to come to stop this problem.

HERE ARE SOME COMMONLY ASKED QUESTIONS:

QUESTION? "WHY IS MY PICTURE "EL FLAT-O?"
ANSWER: *" Your picture is flat, because the objects you draw has dimension to it."*
QUESTION? "WHAT IS DIMENSION?"
"Remember the 'art house?" well this is the 'concrete floor' and the foundation to this 'house."
ANSWER: *"Height Width and Depth"*
QUESTION: "DOES PAPER HAVE DIMENSION?"
ANSWER: *"Yes it has two dimensions: Height, & Width."*
QUESTION: "HOW DO I GET DEPTH OR THREE DIMENSIONS ON A FLAT, TWO DIMENSIONAL PIECE OF PAPER?
ANSWER: *"Perspective!"*
QUESTION: "WHAT IS PERSPECTIVE?"
ANSWER: *"The ability of taking a 3-dimensional object (H,W,D) on a two dimensional piece of paper (H, & W) and make it look like the object is going back or coming forward which will give it a sense of being real and 'touchable.'*
QUESTION: "HOW DO I DO THIS?"
ANSWER: *"There are many steps to this answer and this is where we will untangle this perplexing proble*

"BASIC RULES DIMENSION

These **'EYE LEVEL'** words are used differently. In the "Camera View" is it HOW you are looking and in the "Horizon Line" it is "WHERE" you are looking.
I will explain more in CHAPTER 8, "HORIZON LINE."

1 Dimension-(no such thing
2 Dimension- H &W
3 Dimension-H,W, & D

VANISHING POINTS
1 Point
2 Point
3 Point

CAMERA VIEW
EYE LEVEL
Birds eye
Worm's eye

HORIZON LINE HOME BASE"
for Vanishing Point's
EYE LEVEL
Birds Eye
Worms Eye

CHAPTER FIVE
THE MAGICAL ILLUSION OF PERSPECTIVE

Did you know that when you draw a 3-dimensional (height, width, depth) object on a flat, 2-dimensional piece of paper that you are performing a *type of magic?*

Just like the magician performing magic tricks when they make their objects appear or disappear, all they are doing is simply using the **WORLD OF ILLUSION** to trick our senses into making their   miraculous feats look real and amazing   .

In art, it is the same principal.

It's all about how to make a 3-D, solid object look REAL on a flat piece of paper.

SO…what is the answer to this "DECEPTIVE" trick?

ANSWER:

This IS NOT the hard core mathematical physics that rocket scientists use to get the space shuttle up.

Simply put, **PHYSICS** is the solid mass that makes up everything.

It is also the study of how things move and the forces in nature that make them move.

AND....SO...??? *How does this pertain to art?*

SO… In the world of art we begin by looking at an object in its entirety which is called … "DIMENSION."

AND WITHOUT DIMENSION, YOU HAVE...

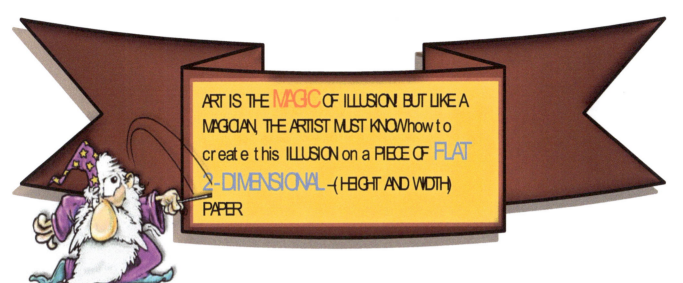

ART IS THE MAGIC OF ILLUSION! BUT LIKE A MAGICIAN, THE ARTIST MUST KNOW how to create this ILLUSION on a PIECE OF FLAT 2-DIMENSIONAL -(HEIGHT AND WIDTH) PAPER

THERE ARE TWO ACTIONS OF DIMENSION
FIRST:
PHYSICAL DIMENSION

SECOND ACTION IS WHAT I WILL CALL:

"IS THERE A ONE DIMENSION?"

No, for all objects that you draw, will have some sort of HEIGHT AND WIDTH, to it (such as a dot, slit, or even the small little period at the end of a sentence… so there is NOT(**that I know of…**) in an ARTISTIC one dimension.

THERE IS:

TWO DIMENSIONS is HEIGHT, AND WIDTH.

The most common two dimensional art objects is a piece of paper or a canvas.

THREE DIMENSION IS: HEIGHT, WIDTH, DEPTH.

This will give the illusion of realism to the

subject that you are drawing on your piece of paper.

Given the subject that you are drawing a THREE DIMENSIONAL look, is usually accomplished by turning your piece at a three- quarter view, and placing it where you can see a side, a top, or bottom depending on how and where you are looking.

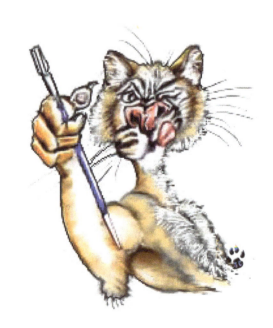

CHAPTER SIX
UNDERSTANDING VANISHING POINTS

I am not going to lie to you…this section is going to be extremely difficult to explain. . *There are many words and actions that piggy back off of each other.*

This section is the "meat and potatoes" of what drawing is all about and without understanding these concepts your drawings will constantly be flat and without life.

This section is like the *"HOLE IN THE BUCKET "SONG,"* It starts out like this:

THE **OBJECT.** *THAT YOU ARE DRAWING* WILL CREATE
THE **DEPTH** LINES.
THE **DEPTH LINES** CREATE THE **VANISHING POINTS.**
THE **HORIZON LINE**..IS CREATED BY WHERE THE **VANISHING POINTS CROSS.**

THE **HEIGHT OF THE HORIZON LINE** FROM THE OBJECT YOU ARE DRAWING IS DETERMINED BY **HOW and WHERE YOU ARE LOOKING AT THIS OBJECT."** WHICH IS CALLED IN *ART TERMS,* **"BIRDS EYE, " "WORMS EYE," OR "EYE LEVEL "**

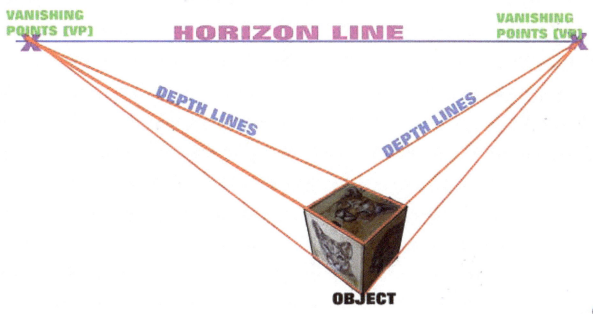

PLEASE DO NOT PANIC !
Even though there are a lot of parts that go into this "SONG," YOU WILL GET IT…this is why this chapter is so important for you to grasp.

So, on the following pages you will see
samples to help explain- in the simplest words I can.
I promise you, you will start to see how this "hole-in-the-bucket" rule works.

THE FIRST QUESTION IS:
WHAT IS THE POSITION OF THE OBJECT?

There are two angles that you will usually see.
(You will notice I am not asking you
where or how you are looking at this box.)

HERE ARE THE "WORDS' TO START MEMORIZING

1. OBJECT
2. DEPTH LINES
3 VANISHING POINTS
4 HORIZON LINE

The *POSITION* of *THE OBJECT* you are looking at is very important in determining the *NUMBER* of *VANISHING POINTS* the object is going to have.

THE ONE POINT
VANISHING POINT

This box has **ONE VANISHING POINT** and is called a "ONE POINT."
AS YOU CAN SEE IN THIS ILLUSTRATION THE DEPTH LINES
WILL ***MEET*** and **CROSS** AT ONE POINT

THIS ACTION NOW HAS **CREATED** THE HORIZON LINE.

IMPORTANT NOTE! THE ONE POINT IS USUALLY FOUND ON OBJECTS THAT ARE *STRAIGHT IN FRONT OF YOU* AND NOT ANGLED

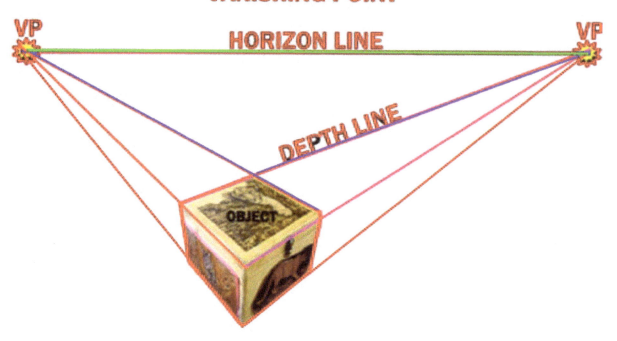

This box has TWO VANISHING POINTS.

Meaning: This box has two sets of **DEPTH LINES** going off the sides of this box.

This is called a: **"TWO POINT."** BECAUSE THIS BOX IS ANGLED...Where you now see a right and left **SIDE** *side* surface of this box and because of this you now are faced with the problem of making the box TWO side surfaces look like they are going back. Thus is the importance of these two sets of depth lines

NOTE: *Unfortunately there is more to this on this particular two vanishing points theory because of the degree of surface you will see on the object..meaning how much surface of the object do you see due to the degree of the ANGLE the box is turned.*

This box ***above*** is equally turned so that you see equal sides on BOTH side planes. These boxes to the right shows the different plane surfaces due to the way they are positioned, which then determines the anlge of the depth lines from wide to narrow.

The illustration of the below boxes is a good example of what the different views of both SIDE AND TOP SURFACE views look like at different heights.

If you were to draw depth lines and establish the horizon lines off of these boxes you would find tthat all the lines goes back to ONE horizon line. But the debth lines will be at different points on the horizon line due to the varied heights and angles of these boxes.   The debth line also will vary in length to the horizon line due to the height and angle of the boxes.   I.E. the top box will have the shortest depth line to the horizon line due to its height. Where as the bottom bigger box will have a longer depth line to the horizon line because it is at the bottom of the stack and you see the most surface area.

SIDE PLANES OF THESE BOXES

Now. to add more fuel to the fire, the DEPTH of the boxes SIDE PLANES also depend o the SIZE of the box and how it's angled.

TOP SURFACES

of these boxes is determined on **WHERE** and **WHAT** position you are at when viewing them. And the side surfaces of the boxes is determined by the degree of angle of each box.

BUT the good news is when ANY OBJECT IS ANGLED no matter the size, or degree of the angle, it WILL BE CONSIDERED A TWO POINT!

This problem will be discussed further on following pages.

NOW I WILL HAVE YOU LOOK AT WHERE AND HOW YOU SEE THIS OBJECT..
which is called **EYE LEVEL** or in my own terminology I use: **"CAMERA VIEW."**

EXPLAINING EYE LEVEL

* **EYE LEVEL** is *WHERE AND HOW* you are looking at the object to establish the **vanishing point- which will create the horizon line- which helps to establish depth of the object.**

For example, where is your body when looking at the object? Are you above the object looking down upon it? Or are you lying flat looking up at it? Or are you looking at the object 'eye to eye..straight on?

I am also going to call "EYE LEVEL" *CAMERA VIEW."*

THIS IS BROKEN DOWN IN THREE CATAGORIES LISTED ON NEXT PAGE

Now, there is plenty more to this eye level thing, of which I will go into deeper detail in chapter Seven, 'The Camera View."

But for right now on the following pages, you will see examples of different views of drawings which will alert you to what you will be facing in chapter seven.

The next page USING THE TABLE EXAMPLE on the next page, shows you how the position of your body determines the SIZE OF THE SURFACE PLANES of the object you are looking at.

EYE LEVEL - The main thing for you to remember is that if you start out at EYE LEVEL with the object (This table ledge for instance) you will see NO PLANE! Just the ledge of the table.

BIRDS EYE - but the **MORE** you stand UP, the **MORE** of the tables surface area you will see, Until you finally will have to be hanging from the chandelier looking down FULLY at the table top to see a *FULL BIRDS EYE VIEW.*

WORMS EYE, This rule goes for WORMS EYE, but you then are sinking to your knees and as you eventually go on your back will see more of the plane until eventually you will be fully under the table looking directly UP at the full surface of the bottom of the table.

1. EYE LEVEL

2. BIRDS EYE

3. WORMS EYE

EXAMPLES OF VANISHING POINTS, AND EYE LEVELS
AKA: VIEW'S, OR CAMERA VIEW

YOUR ORDINARY ONE (VANISHING) POINT

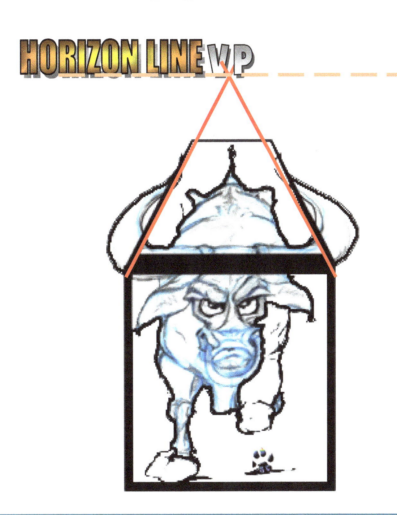

THIS IS A ONE POINT

It is a simple box that has one set of depth lines going straight back but narrowing until they cross.. When they do this, they have just formed a **'VANISHING POINT.'** The 'VANISHING POINT' OR 'VP", has just established the **HORIZON LINE.**
The HORIZON LINE has just established the depth of the subject.

(NOTE: this is just an example of a __ONE POINT__, I am not stating what degree (where you are looking at) EYE LEVEL This will be explained further in this chapter.)

EYELEVEL TWO POINT

THIS VIEW IS A EYE LEVEL, TWO POINT,

This view is usually achieved by angling the object and sitting down and pointing the camera right at the corner edge of the object and obliterating the view of the top of the object.

This two point view will STILL have <u>two sets</u> of depth lines coming off the BOTTOM and TOP EDGES of the object. But being as there is no top view then these depth lines are only going to give the perspective distance of the SIDES (or planes) of the object ONLY!!!

This view is not a popular one because of the absence of the top of the object and without that top view the drawing usually gives the illusion of being flat.

This drawing is an EQUAL view where you are only seeing TWO sides of the object, and NO TOP and it would be the skill of shading and correct perspective depths of the two side planes that will make this particular view believable.

The distance usually to get this view would be approximately two to four feet away.

ONE POINT, TWO POINT, THREE POINT BIRDS EYE

This piece is a bit of a difficult one because there are many **DEPTH LINES** that goes off of this piece…I haven't put them ALL in because of the restrictions of this paper..But what you are looking at is a:, ONE POINT, TWO POINT, THREE POINT, BIRDS EYE.

1. the cup and box is viewed as a BIRDS EYE because your VIEW is looking DOWN upon it, (this is not a full birds eye, because you can not see the full bottom of the cup and the top of the cup is not a full circle, but just off of being a perfect circle.

1.THE BOTTOM BOX is in at ¾ angle where you see two sets of DEPTH LINES going off the top and bottom of the box

3. It is classified as a THREE POINT because there is another set of DEPTH LINES going down giving the viewer the sense of looking from top of the cup down to the distant floor.

(FAVORITE OF THE COMIC BOOK ARTISTS.)

EYE LEVEL

This view is straight on…looking eye to eye with the subject, you do not see top of body or underneath just 'face on!"

This view is usually used a lot by portrait artists, because most of the time it's more important to get the features of the face than a composition of the full body.

A cartoonists would take the protrusions that come out at the object and exaggerate them in order to make the cartoon object funny, and perspectivly feeling as though it is IN YOUR FACE and coming out toward you.

TWO POINT -1/4 BIRDS EYE

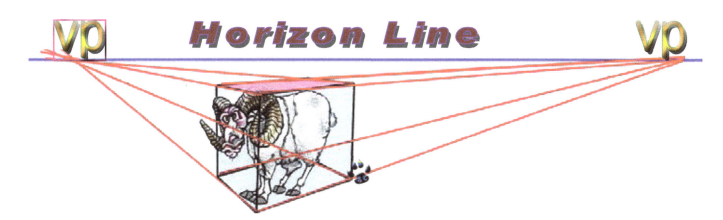

This VIEW is a two point, 1/4 birds eye view this VIEW is now where you are stepping back about three to five feet and seeing more of the side of the ram's body and not much of his back. You are pretty level with him and not much taller than him either. You don't see much of his back. He is standing at a ¾ view forcing you once again to see him as a "boxy' mass, which means he will be considered a TWO POINT = "VP")

Notice the top surface of this box *which I have tinted pink*. See how narrow it is…this gives you the AMOUNT OF VIEW of the back of the ram. This gives you the amount of surface the BIRDS EYE VIEW you are looking at. Notice too, the SMALL distance above the ram where the horizon line is. This is also a way to judge your percentage of the birds-eye view you are looking at.

The _LOWER_ the horizon line the _LESS_ you will see of the _TOP_ of the object. THE HIGHER the horizon line goes means the _MORE_ you are going to see the _TOP_ of the object.

Hint: *the larger the top surface of the "boxy mass" the higher you are to the object seeing more of the TOP of the object… The less you see of the top surface of the "boxy mass" the smaller BIRDS EYE VIEW you'll see.*

This view is one of the most common that artists draw because it is simple to render and it is the most successful in getting your piece to look as natural as possible on the two dimensional paper.

TWO POINT
1/2 BIRDS EYE VIEW

This view is the most used, and most popular because usually your position to the object is about four to six feet away, and usually taken while sitting or crouching just above the object.

The reason why it's a half birds eye is because you are seeing a little more than a fourth, and a little less than three quarters TOP surface view. (Shaded in light blue.)

The object is usually placed on a table or bench.

It is this view that gives the most surface information on the objects three sides. (Usually the fourth side is not seen no matter what angle that this object is placed in.)

2 POINT, 3/4 BIRDS EYE VIEW

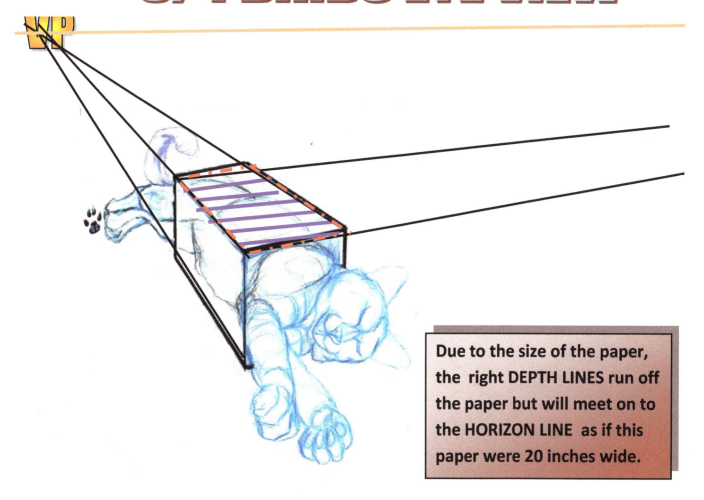

Due to the size of the paper, the right DEPTH LINES run off the paper but will meet on to the HORIZON LINE as if this paper were 20 inches wide.

This view is another most common because of the top of the 'box' (shaded in purple lines) you will see most of the object. This is why I call it this view a ¾ *BIRDS EYE VIEW.*

It is as though you are kneeling but your back is straight, but, you are a bit of a distance away from the cat which prevents you from looking directly down upon the animal, but yet you can see most of the top and side planes of the animal.

This view is used constantly because it tells ALMOST a *'complete story'* in its composition.

Also look at the distance of the horizon line to the cat in the box..it's higher meaning now that you are seeing MORE of the cat's side and top.

3/4 (ALMOST FULL) BIRDS-EYE, TWO POINT, THREE POINT

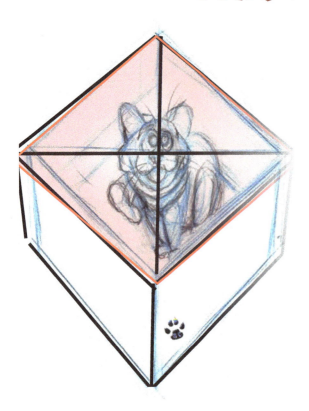

This VIEW is A 3 POINT, TWO POINT, ¾ BIRDS EYE because the VIEW is not quite a fully over the top of the box.

It is as though the viewer has stepped back just a bit from fully looking over the top of the box.

But yet they can see almost 99% of the bottom of this box and the cat. (see sample "A")Where as in sample "B" one can see fully OVER the top of the cat this is a sample of a FULL BIRDS EYE. (in this case this fat cat is hiding the FULL bottom of the box.

This VIEW is a pretty common one, especially if the artist is conveying a thought of something deep in a box, or hole. This VIEW is used quite frequently with comic book, graphic illustrators, cartoonists, etc. to get a dramatic effect.

FULL BIRDS EYE VIEW

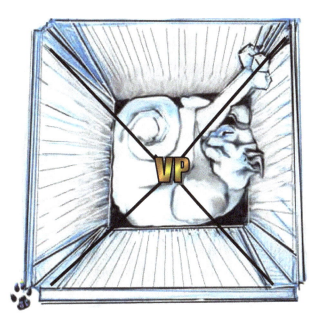

You are now looking straight down into the object. You will not see the outside sides of the object. But just the inside sides and bottom. In this VIEW it will go from large (the top of the box) to small which gives the illusion of deep DEPTH.

This VIEW is difficult to do because if not shaded right, or, drawn correctly, the picture can look flat. So, one has to render the line work with large to small VIEW in mind., and be aware of the correct slant of the corner lines(if you are drawing a box.) as well as be mindful of the lighting source that will also give it the sense of DEPTH.

This view is not used that much unless the artist is attempting to make a dramatic point such as looking in a well, or a coffin, or looking into a grave, or deep hole..

This view is mostly used by comic book, cartoonists, graphic novel, sci-fi, fantasy, and animation artists.

THIS VIEW IS A 2 POINT, 1/8 WORMS EYE

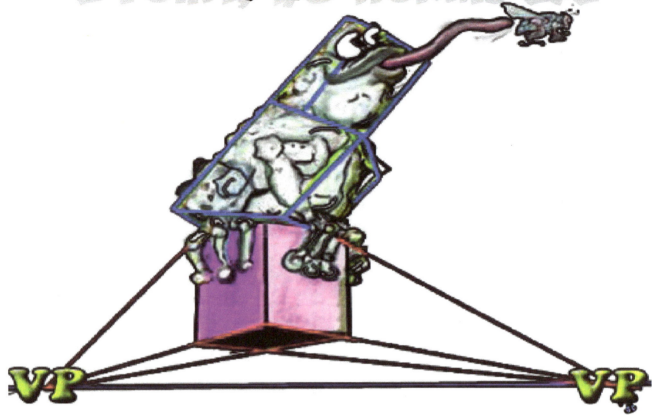

This view is not a common one, and you usually see it used when one is trying to capture a scene where you are not quite eye level with your subject but are looking under and UP just a bit.

The "1/8" view of the box is in black..this worms eye is now where you are going to start looking UNDER and UP! The bottom surface plane of the object is going to be doing the same fractional view…(1/8,1/4.1/2,/3/4 and full) as the BIRDS EYE, but now you are looking UP instead of DOWN!

The horizon line rule is going to be just the same as the BIRDS EYE, meaning that the DISTANCE from the object will tell you how much surface area you are viewing..REMEMBER: IF THE HORIZON LINE IS CLOSEST TO THE OBJECT you will be seeing LESS of the surface plane, and as you are seeing MORE of the surface plane, the FURTHER AWAY THE HORIZON LINE IS GOING TO MOVE!

This view is used quite a bit with the comic book, graphic novel, and children book illustrators.

ONE POINT 3/4 WORMS EYE

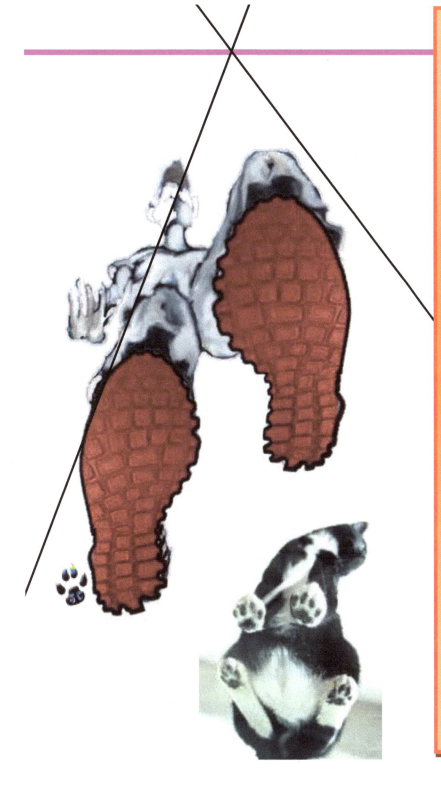

This view is as though you are looking up through a piece of glass.

It is not a full worms eye, because if it was then all you would see would be the full soles of the shoes and maybe the palm of the hand, the outline of the pants, shirt and maybe the tip of the baseball cap..and this would not make compositional sense.

It is a tool that comic book, graphic artists, cartoonists, fantasy, and sci-fi

THIS is a ONE POINT, TWO POINT, EYE LEVEL MULTIBLE VIEW POINTS

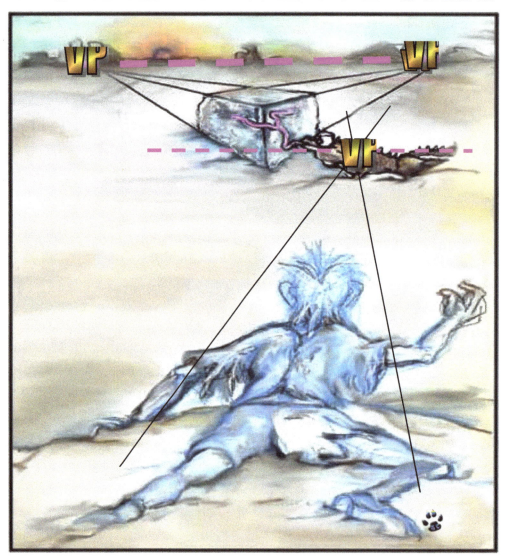

This VIEW has two HORIZON LINES because of the positions of the two major objects (which is the man and the ice cube.)

I call this a ONE POINT (man) TWO POINT (ice cube), EYE LEVEL (lizard)…3/4 SEMI BIRDS EYE (LOOKING DOWN UPON THE MAN.) This is a MULTIPLE EYE VIEW on all subjects, and can be quite a confusing composition to beginners.

This is a view that photographers pick up quite a lot, depending on where they are standing or what they are standing on in order to get an angled ¾ bird's eye or worm's eye. It is something that beginners should practice on when they get the other views down pat.

CHAPTER SEVEN
CAMERA VIEW
MORE DETAILS ABOUT EYE LEVELS AND VIEWS

I am going to use the term **"CAMERA VIEW"** to help the artist when they are using a PICTURE that you find in a magazine, book or on line.

When you are looking at a picture, the CAMERA VIEW is the simplest way to show you where the EYE LEVELS (BIRDS, WORMS and STRAIGHT ON-(called " EYE LEVEL")) has been established and where and how the photographer has positioned themselves in the picture.

The second reason I use this term *"CAMERA VIEW"* is as a reference to help the artist that wants to draw from real life using no camera, but when they look at the scene they can imagine that it's their EYES that will view the scenery as if they are looking through a camera.

This will help the artist establish their viewing position and help to establish the correct *EYE LEVELS.*

Which in the art language is called *"BIRDS EYE," "WORMS EYE," and "EYE LEVEL."* (which is looking at an object 'eye to eye, or straight on.)

So, let's think about this a bit. When you are out taking pictures and you want to get a certain shot you have to position your body in such a way in order to get that shot, right?

Drawing scenes in art is no different. In order to get that certain shot, you have to position your body in such a way to get that special shot you want to draw.

Again, this is called *EYE LEVEL.*

Because, you are positioning your body to get the angle of the object and you will be using your eyes as though you are looking through a camera.

Next we resolve how to get what you have seen, (or see) onto the flat two dimensional piece of paper ... which is going back to the same issue of DIMENSION (height, width, depth which establishes PERSPECTIVE.

This is the 'hole-in-the-bucket" talkled about in chapter 6.

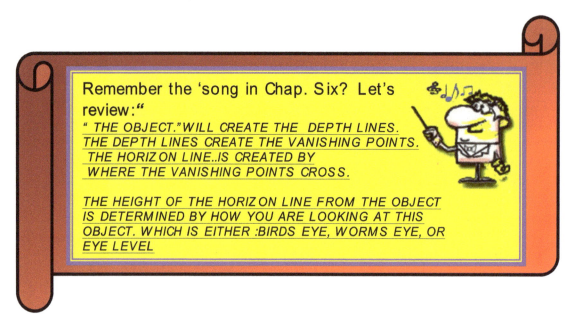

Remember the 'song in Chap. Six? Let's review:"
" THE OBJECT."WILL CREATE THE DEPTH LINES.
THE DEPTH LINES CREATE THE VANISHING POINTS.
THE HORIZON LINE..IS CREATED BY
WHERE THE VANISHING POINTS CROSS.

THE HEIGHT OF THE HORIZON LINE FROM THE OBJECT IS DETERMINED BY HOW YOU ARE LOOKING AT THIS OBJECT. WHICH IS EITHER :BIRDS EYE, WORMS EYE, OR EYE LEVEL

The *DIFFERENCE* in this chapter is **REALITY VS. PHOTOGRAPH** and how you will be able to interpret both scenarios and draw them accurately.

The term **EYE LEVEL** is the real snake in the grass!

Remember back in Chapter Four, in "EL FLATO?" And the last two steps were:

Camera View
Eye Level
Bird's Eye
Worms Eye

Horizon Line
Eye Level
Birds Eye
Worms Eye

"THE MAGIC OF FOUR"

This is where everything starts getting confusing because there are two EYE LEVELS.

The **ACTION** of the *EYE LEVELS* in **BOTH STEPS** are basically the same because they involve eyeball "Action" meaning, *"WHERE YOU ARE LOOKING AT THE OBJECT."*

The **DIFFERENCE** between CAMERA VIEW "EYE LEVEL" and HORIZON EYE LEVEL is:

1. "CAMERA VIEW" EYE LEVEL:
IT IS the **CAMERA** that is **ESTABLISHING THE EYE LEVEL** **BY YOU** *a*s a photographer when you are pointing and shooting at this object in a position that pleases you and getting the exact picture you want, as if you are shooting from a ladder, or lying on the floor looking up at the object or straight on.

2. HORIZON EYE LEVEL :
The "HORIZON LINE" EYE LEVEL is an **ESTABLISHED** LINE *from the STATIC CHOSEN object* that has been selected by either by the artist's eyes or camera. And then through DRAWING DEPTH LINES OFF of this object.to where these DEBTH LINES meet and cross, which then will establish the "VANISHING POINTS" which CREATES the HORIZON LINE !

Remember this clue -Always ask yourself this question, "WHERE ARE YOU WHEN YOU ARE LOOKING AT THE OBJECT?."

By doing this you will become aware of what EYELEVEL you are LOOKING AT…meaning…
BIRDS EYE
WORMS EYE

* STRAIGHT ON EYE LEVEL * NOTE:(This eyelevel *YOU CAN NOT RUN DEPTH LINES off of because there is NO TOP OR BOTTOM PLANES* in which to run these lines off of.
Remember, the object WILL NOT be ANGLED!--- It is STRAIGHT ON so you see only ONE plane! (See the 'table top' theory in chapter 6 if you need to refresh your mind on the different levels you are viewing your object at.)

Now we have to deal with two more problems
1. LOOKING AT SOMETHING REAL
2. LOOKING AT A PICTURE

So again…what does this mean?

On the next page you will see a man and a cat, a snake and the snake charmer. THEY ARE LOOKING AT something **REAL!!**

Both of these drawings represent the characters natural EYE LEVEL. One is standing and the rest of the characters are sitting… or coiled.

All of these characters are naturally focusing on objects out in front of them. They are not focusing on an object that is on the ground or above them but **IN FRONT OF THEM.**

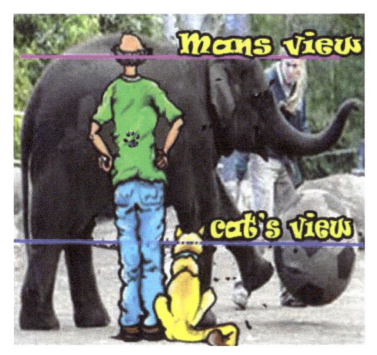

For the man and the cat because of their height and positions they have taken..one standing the other sitting, their EYE LEVEL when looking STRAIGHT AHEAD is where they have established THEIR HORIZON LINE!

For snake and snake charmer, This is An established natural EYE LEVEL because they are looking EQUALLY at one another

For no matter what their body positions are, they are looking straight ahead of them and this will automatically set up the horizon line.

That step is pretty simple…NOW…

LOOKING AT A PICTURE

This next step is a bit harder to explain because it involves what position the object is being viewed at and where the object is when getting its picture taken.

You need to KNOW how the photographer's body was positioned when the picture was taken. Were they kneeling, sitting, standing, standing on a ladder or lying down and looking up at the object? Are they on their side, stomach or back?

And another factor to figure in is: HOW FAR AWAY was the photographer when they took the shot.

There are clues that will help you establish these questions… the major clue is: **LOOKING AT THE TOP SURFACE OF THE OBJECT.**

Your question that you should ask yourself is: "**WHAT AND HOW DO I SEE OF THE OBJECTS TOP SURFACE?** Is it, non- existent? Or do I see a small amount of the top of the surface? Or do I see a lot of the top surface of the object?"

There are clues that will help you establish these questions… the major clue is: LOOKING AT THE TOP SURFACE OF THE OBJECT.

Your question that you should ask yourself is: "What and How do I see of the objects top surface? Is it, non- existent? Or do I see a small amount of the top of the surface? Or do I see a lot of the top surface of the object?"

LOOKING AT THE AMOUNT OF PLANES AS A FRACTION

To make this easier for you to follow and instead of asking you HOW MUCH of the surface do you see every time you look at a picture, I have put these views in simple mathematical fractions. To help you estimate the amount of top surface you are seeing.

The fractional table will look like this:

{
(Looking straight at the object is called;)
EYE LEVEL

1/8 .- 1/4 - ½ ¾

Extreme views are called:
FULL BIRDS EYE &
WORMS EYE
}

The extreme view of FULL BIRDS EYE and WORMS EYE are where you do not see the sides of the object but JUST the top (BIRDS EYE) or the bottom of the object (WORMS EYE.)

SO….when using a PICTURE… The photographer has done all the work for you by establishing

what I call a: *CAMERA VIEW HORIZON LINE.*

You then have to establish where he was aiming or focusing his camera at, as well as figure out where he was standing, and what position he was in. (Which in this case was standing off to the left hand side

Then when you figure out the main object the photographer was focusing on then as an artist and a sluth, you take that object and draw depth lines off of this main object WHICH WILL ESTABLISH THE HORIZON LINE and proceed to draw your masterpiece from the clues that have already been established FOR you by the camera, and taking this stationary picture to draw PHYSICAL depth lines from…and get an accurate horizon line from where upon then you can use the horizon line as an ancor to draw the rest of your picture accurately.

REAL VIEW NOT A TAKEN BY A CAMERA… This is a bit more nvolved, this will entail a REAL OBJECT that YOU are focusing on and no camera is involved.

In other words there are a few questions that will be asked
#1 question : **"WHAT IS YOUR POSITION TO THE OBJECT? AND HOW FAR AWAY OR NEAR THE OBJECT ARE YOU TO THE OBJECT?**

"The answer is: Look at the angle and height of the object that you have focused on.
In this case in this picture, I have the man looking at the corner of the house but I can imagine him across the street and the house maybe 50 more feet further back from the street near the back of the property which will make the house smaller in order to get this view..
And because the house is smaller indicating a distance away from the drawn man.)I have made this illusion more believable because I have drawn the man bigger and "IN YOUR FACE!" So, now you take out your sketch book and YOU as the artist will then have to establish.

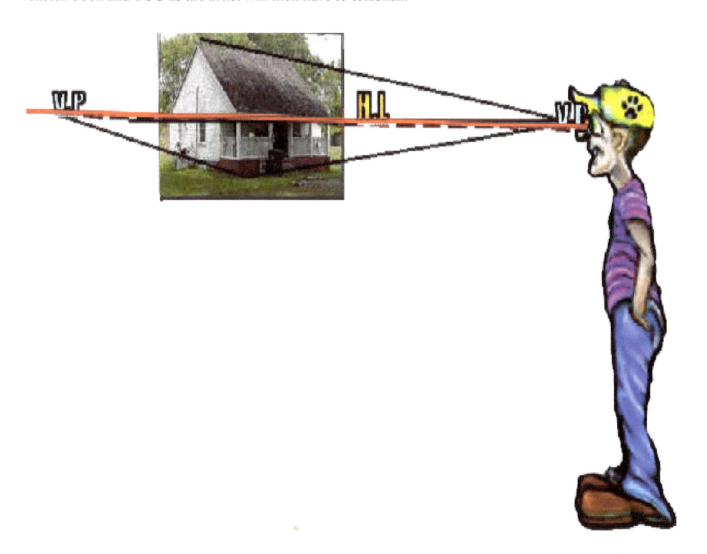

2 question : **WHERE AND WHAT PERCENTAGE OF THE MAIN SURFACE DO I SEE AND WHAT EYE LEVEL** (birds, worms, or straight on eye level am I looking at

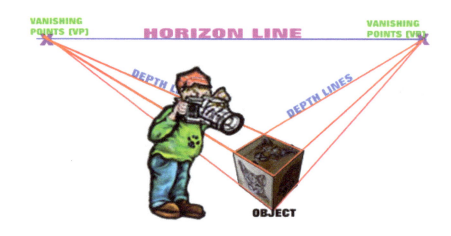

In this picture I see a LOT of the roof about ¾ percentage and the same percentage of the front side of the house. Where as I am seeing maybe ½ percentage of the left side of the house that is turned away from me. Bringing up the next question…

#3 QUESTION, THEN HOW MANY V.P. AM I SEEING HERE? 1 point? Two point? Three point?..

This house is NOT a three point birds eye because you are NOT LOOKING DOWN or are you FLYING OVER this house.

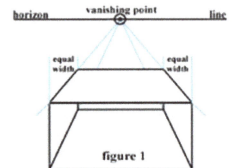

Or are you lying on your back Looking UP at this house as in a worms eye view.

The house is NOT straight on, making it a ONE POINT where the depth lines would be going straight back

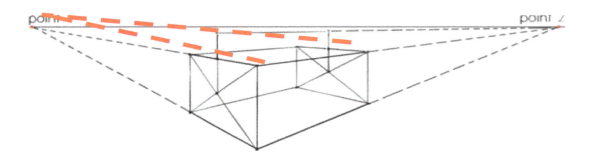

But this house is **ANGLED** giving you a **TWO POINT** perspective where you will have TWO vanishing pints coming off the eve of the roof and the sides and bottom of the house as you can see in the illustration. NOW…to make things a bit more confusing you will see that I've drawn just a few depth lines coming off of the front and left side of the house. It will be ASSUMUED that there is a depth line coming off the bottom of the RIGHT side of the house that will go towards the LEFT side of the horizon line. this is because this side of the house can not be seen…*REMEMBER this house is a BOX. And is to be treated as such…*

#4TH QUESTION: HOW DO I ESTABLISH THE HORIZON LINE?

To answer that, invision this house as a BOX where then you can draw the the depth lines going off the main part of the house and part of the roof.

Now I can hear you ask.."UMMMM why do I only see the depth lines going off of the FRONT half of this house? And not the back half." This is because as you can see if you were to draw a depth line coming off the back half SLANT (shown in PINK!) that this line WILL NOT match up to the left VP. BUT never fear, it's the BOTTOM of the back side EVE of the roof that will match to the left VP.and as you can see that these bottom eves of both front and back of the house IS the HORIZON LINE.

ALSO as a clue when you draw the house you can use the depth of the front of the house's roof as a guide line to judge the width of the back side, but it's the SLANT of the non VP portion of this roof that will give you the proper ANGLE to make a correct proportional drawing.
 roof and the bottom and opposite side of of this house to where all the depth lines will meet and cross. YOU HAVE JUST ESTABLISHED THE HORIZON LINE FROM A REAL OBJECT.

SOME MORE INFORMATION ON THE NATURAL WAY THAT YOU LOOK AT A SUBJECT USING YOUR EYEBALLS INSTEAD OF A CAMERA.

In these next pages you will see that I will keep repeating these steps because I want to get firmly established into your mind HOW, WHAT, and WHY.

Important Point One is simply where you are looking. You aren't paying any attention to establish any-thing. You are just wandering through life taking all the sights in and enjoying what you are seeing.

SO HOW DO YOU START THIS PROCESS?

 You start by asking these questions: "*RELATIVE TO WHERE I'M STANDING, AND THE ANGLE I'M STANDING, THEN WHAT VIEW I AM LOOKING AT? (EYE LEVEL BIRDS EYE? OR WORMS EYE?)* and what angle is the object? Is it at an angle or is it a straight on view meaning that I am standing in FRONT of this object?This is where you start being conscience of your position and how far away you are as you are looking at the scenes.

"Where and what objects do I use the depth lines in order to establish my HORIZON LINE?"

"How much surface of the object am I seeing in these views?"

"And, what fraction of the views I am seeing? (1/8, ¼, ½ ¾ view.)"

BUT this philosophy will change the minute you want to draw the scene you are looking at, and you set up your easel to start drawing your masterpiece. NOW you are looking at an alive scene which is subject to light changing, and other things that could change the mood and perspective of your scene. BUT the concept of using your EYEBALLS is the same as if you are going to use a camera to freeze your scene.

 For example on the next pages are scenes that you could be seeing on your travels or walks and you are looking at because they are interesting, and you want to draw them from life,. You have your easel on your back, and drawing materials in hand, and you want to capture what you SEE by your EYES!

HOUSE

1. If you determined, for the house, a ½ birds eye because you are seeing what I call an "AVERAGE" VIEW of the surface of the roof and the horizon line is established at the EDGE OF THE WINDOW You are correct. (To make sure of this, draw the DEPTH LINES coming off the roof and see where they meet, which will establish the HORIZON LINE. which in this case is the edge of the bottom of the window.

And if you figured out where you would be if you were looking at this house you would be correct in assuming you are about 50 feet away because the house itself is small, and you are positioned a bit off the center of the house to the left.

CAMEL 2. If you came up with a slight BIRDS EYE with the camel, you would be correct. Because you are looking at a slight angle about 10 to 15 feet away from it, and a bit to the right side NOT straight on.

The giveaway is that the legs of this camel do have depth to them because of the ANGLE they are at.
 If you drew depth lines from these legs, you would see that the HORIZON LINE is a spot just above the camels head and just below the lower part of the ridge, which makes this view a 1/4 BIRDS EYE. (the amount the top of the camel's head, and the distance between the camels front and back legs, which I don't see much plane. This gives me this fraction.
But yet, the camel itself is almost at an EYE LEVEL which makes this picture a bit of an anomaly and to the untrained eye this could be a confusing factor, this is the reason why one has to look at this camel as a RECTANGLE SHAPE which helps to establish depth.

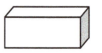

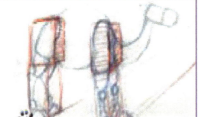

This view is a confusing one and seemingly a conundrum..But, I will help your confusion by bringing out one important fact that you MUST realize that this camel has depth, and is a solid **3-DIMENSIONAL** animal. and you must see this animal as a solid mass!

So if I were to block this animal in using shapes, where will the depth lines go on these shapes? This is what I call the "GLASS GHOST THEORY" and I will be discussing this further in chapter 20.

HAMBURGERS

3. In this burger scene, If you guessed that the overall scene that you are viewing is a 3/4 BIRDS EYE view you are correct. TO A POINT...BECAUSE...these juicy burgers have a multitude of fractional BIRDS EYE views, BECAUSE...of the layered DISTANCE OF THE BURGERS that are from the CAMERA VIEW.

The **_further away_** the burgers are to the camera, the SMALLER and MORE NARROW the oval shape becomes, and as you can see the closer the burgers are to the photographer the BIGGER the surface of the bun is...this is what I am saying about the height of the horizon line will dictate the surface's plane sizes.

Usually the first thought that comes into your mind is: "my brain going to explode here with the confusions of this view and it's too much 'eyeballing confusing scenes!"

Never fear! Just slow down and
really look at this scene...and then
yourself 'what is the first thing that I see?
If you really look, you will see how all the burgers are lined up like soldiers in review that are standing on a hill.

And where does your eye lead? They go UP!
And what do you do to establish a HORIZON LINE?

*You put in DEPTH LINES. And where they cross is where
he HORIZON LINE is established.(Which in this picture the horizon line is too far above and runs off the
page, so ust imagine the yellow lines going up until hey cross this is where the HORIZON line will be established, telling you WHERE the camera is that is taking this picture..which is
next to the closest burger in blue...and above it.)*

BUT...this doesn't solve the multi-layered surface views does it? And how are you going to draw these things correctly, and in the right perspective?

WELL...you can see that the burgers differ in heights right? The front burger (in blue) is "in your face!" meaning it's closest to you so the top of the is bigger than the rest of the burgers.

Now take a look at the burgers ringed in green, pink and red, you see that all these 'ovals' are getting more squashed, because they are all going away from you, thus, you see less of the surface of the buns. The DEPTH LINES also are a big hint for they go from wide to narrow.

BEACH SCENE

4. In this beach scene, if you said that this view starts out as a ¾ BIRDS EYE but then when it goes way back it becomes **ALMOST** an EYE LEVEL you are correct.

In order to get this view, you are standing on a small hill and looking straight ahead of you. Your peripheral vision is taking in the WIDE bottom portion of the sand, even though you are looking straight ahead. This is because your vision is closest to this part of the beach and you are seeing a lot of the plane's surface.

This is what I call *"IN YOUR FACE!"* Because it is the FIRST THING YOU SEE. and it is going to be the BIGGEST! BIG TO SMALL as you can see what is happening in this shot.

This view again, I will call a multi-fractional view that goes from ¾ BIRDS EYE, (because in your periferial vision is looking DOWN upon this widest portion of the sandy beach.

Then as the beach goes back more you can see that it is beginning to get ever smaller…This is the reason why I have tagged the fracional incraments from ¾, to ½ to 1/8 view and then to a flat EYE LEVEL. (but when you draw this just look at the overall picture as a wide **INVERTED "V"**)

The horizon line is established where the sandy shore line meets the hills: because the **DEPTH LINES** start from where you are standing, and go back and cross at that point.

Dancers

5. The last example is now you are at a play, and you are about twenty or thirty feet away and your positions is standing on the middle rungs of a LADDER looking straight at these dancers.

So, if you say that this picture is a straight on **EYE LEVEL** you hit the jackpot!

The **HORIZON LINE** is straight through the lady's waist line, because your focus is obviously right on the lady and her waist line, as well as the sailors on the right and left of her. (Hint to help you with your depth of the back sailors..look where their heads are in relationship to the ladies elbow.)

You see no depth lines going anywhere because there is nothing to draw the depth line from, meaning that there is no "V" (as you saw in the beach scene,) to indicate the dancers in a different formation other than this straight line. Even the sailors in the back are in a straight line and are smaller because the are in the back. ***LARGE TO SMALL!***

BUT...this view has more to it than what you see…and it all centers around depth of the front dancers to the back dancers…but to keep it in a '***SIMPLE SAM"*** description, just remember ***LARGE to small!*** *as objects move BACK.*

Girl dancer: **IN YOUR FACE,** Back dancers **RECEDING** away from you, they will be smaller. This will give you depth to your picture if you were to draw it.

(the photographer is in FRONT of these dancers)

EYEBALLS vs CAMERA...THE SAME PRINCIPALS

The examples on the other pages were as if you were using your EYEBALLS to draw a scene from (as if you were to set up an easel at the scene and start drawing!!! (even though these were samples from pictures, BOTH EYEBALL and CAMERA theory use the same principal.)

You will be using the same concepts as IF YOU WERE seeing the scene thru a CAMERA, instead of your eyeballs. But the nice thing about using a camera is that you take these pictures back to your studio to draw from.

The rules are the same as if you were using your eyeballs. But this time you have a picture that isn't going to change in lighting or the scenery moving on you…You can take your time to draw your masterpiece.

The CAMERA will be now your 'eyeballs' and how you get your shots depends on how you are going to position your body.

This point is the major key to understanding CAMERA VIEW.

In order to make sure you REALLY understand this I will once again REVIEW the TABLE TOP THEORY found in Chapter six.

But this time I will make a 'game' of it, to make sure that you will not forget WHAT the EYE LEVELS are that pertain to the EYEBALL and CAMERA VIEW rules,

And knowing this, helps you keep in mind HOW it effects the SIZE of the surfaces of your object.

And WHERE your position is when you are looking at this object…

all of these 'rules' need to get straight in your mind in order to really understand PERSPECTIVE.

TABLE TOP REVIEW

So, let's play a game.
 You are a photographer. And you read in an art/photography magazine that will pay you $2000.00 for the best and most unusual views of an ordinary piece of furniture which will be a table.

The rules are simple…you just have to photograph this table in 10 positional shots. (I'm omitting 1/8 view as you see in the above table, for you will get the idea thru these 10 views)

1 EYE LEVEL BIRDS EYE (THIS WILL BE THE SAME
AS THE EYE LEVEL WORMS EYE. SEE NO TOP OR BOTTOM. OF
TABLE.)
2. 1/8 BIRDS EYE
3 1/4 BIRD'S EYE'VIEW
4. ½ BIRD'S EYE'VIEWS
5 ¾ BIRD'S EYE VIEW
6 A FULL BIRD'S EYE VIEW

6. EYE LEVEL WORMS EYE(THIS WILL BE THE SAME
AS THE EYE LEVEL BIRDS EYE. SEE NO TOP OR BOTTOM OF
TABLE.)
7. 1/8TH
8. 1/4
9. 1/2
10. 3/4
ARE THE SAME AS THE BIRDS EYE BUT
YOU WILL BE CROUCHING INSTEAD OF STANDING
10. FULL WORMS EYE YOU ARE COMPLETELY UNDER THE
TABLE LOOKING UP.

I WILL OMIT THE 4 STEPS THAT YOU SEE IN THE BIRDS EYE BECAUSE
THEY ARE THE SAME STEPS EXCEPT YOU ARE CROUCHING INSTEAD OF STANDING.
SO I WILL SHOW YOU THE FIRST AND LAST STEP OF THE WORMS EYE.

Now, you've already seen examples of these views in the vanishing point chapter, but, your question now should be: "OK, just HOW do I get these views?"

STEP 1 BIRDS EYE LEVEL

1. Choose an end of the table, it doesn't matter which end.

2. Bend just a bit until you see JUST THE MIDDLE OF THE LEDGE of the table.

3. You will NOT SEE the TOP of the table,

4. You will not see the underneath part of the table.

5. The Horizon line is now in the middle of the edge you are looking at.

To make this simple, ALL the table examples will be ONE POINT.

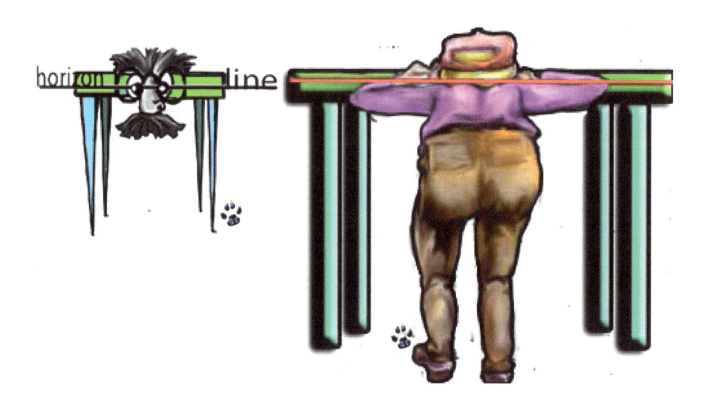

STEP 2
THE 1/8th BIRDS EYE VIEW

1. Straighten out your back just a little bit.

2. You are starting to see A SMALL PORTION of the TOP of the table.

3. The horizon line is now just starting to rise off the middle ledge, and it is about 2-4 inches above the top of the table

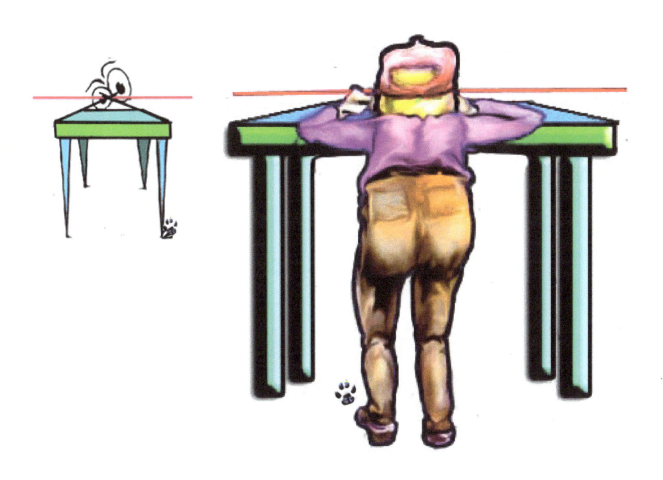

STEP 3
THE 1/4h BIRDS EYE VIEW

1. Straighten out your back to just a bit more

2. You are starting to see a bit more of the TOP of the table.

3. The far end of the table is still pretty far off, and the horizon line has now risen to about just about 8 to 10 inches from the end of the table.

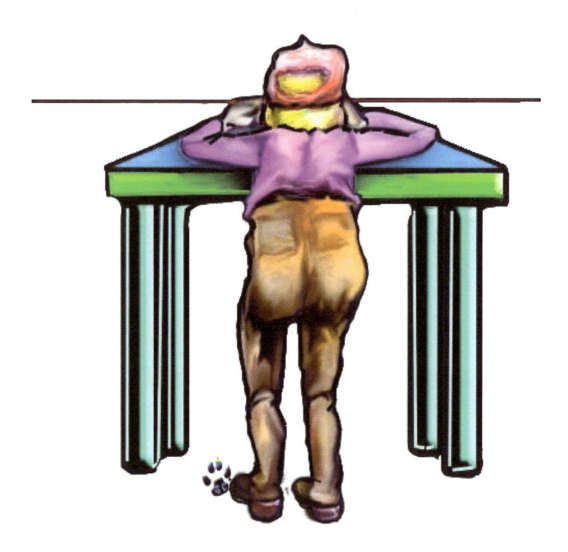

STEP 4
½ BIRD'S EYE VIEW

This view is usually the most common to see and draw because it's what you observe most naturally without bending or standing on a ladder. A lot of times this view is done by sitting down. comfortably with your back straight. But for this exersise you will:

1. STAND UP and move back from the table about 4 feet or more

2. Notice now how much of the top of the table you are seeing.

3. The FURTHER BACK YOU GO, the bigger and MORE of the tables surface you will see.

4. The Horizon line is now about two to two and half feet up and off the back of the table.

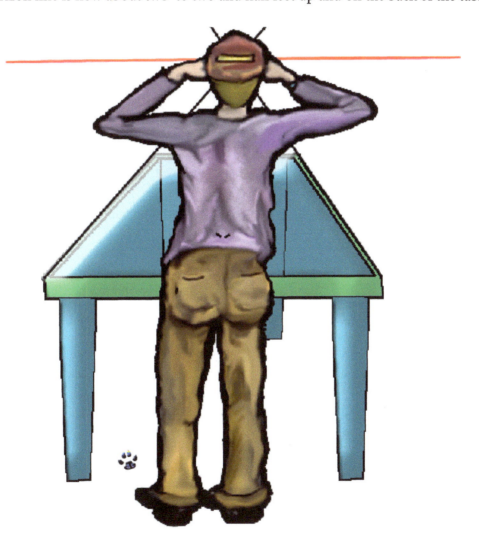

STEP 5
3/4 BIRD'S EYE VIEW

1. Get a step stool or small ladder to give you height (unless you are 7 feet tall!)
2. Place the ladder about 2 feet away from the table
3. Lean as far over the table as you can to where
you will be able to get as much f the table as you can but not quite the full flat plane as if you were looking at the table hanging from the middle of the ceiling hanging on a chandelier over the table.

This view the table will still **NOT** have the perfect equal square look.
But look like the sample in red

4. The horizon line is now shifted to where it is starting to rise over the table into a pyramid shape and it's over your head, but it's not quite over the center of the table.

SIDE VIEW OF WHAT THE DEPTH LINES LOOK LIKE AT A FULL BIRD'S EYE VIEW

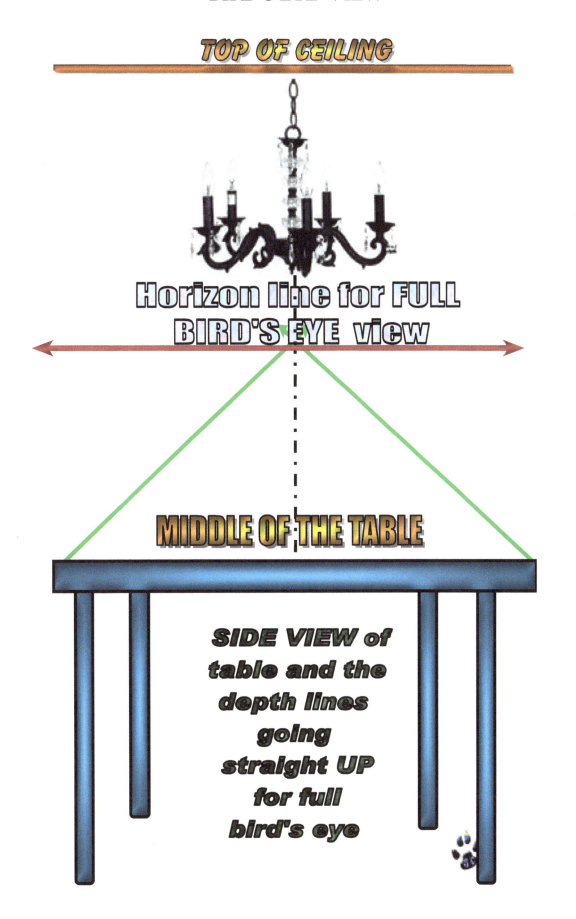

STEP 6
FULL BIRD'S EYE

1. Now you will pretend that you are an eagle and you are flying over the table and when you lo down, you will see JUST THE FULL TOP OF THE TABLE, and you will NOT SEE any of the sides of the table.

2. The depth lines now have shifted into a pyramid where they cross directly over the table.

Another way to look at this FULL BIRDS EYE is as if you were pasted onto the top portion of the wall, with your back flat up against the ceiling. The table is next to the wall too, so that your view is directly over the top of the table. Thus you can see the pyramid effect of the depth lines.

This is the view and shape of the table now you are seeing in a full birds eye.

The star is the middle of the table where your eyes are now glued to.

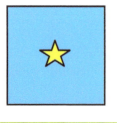

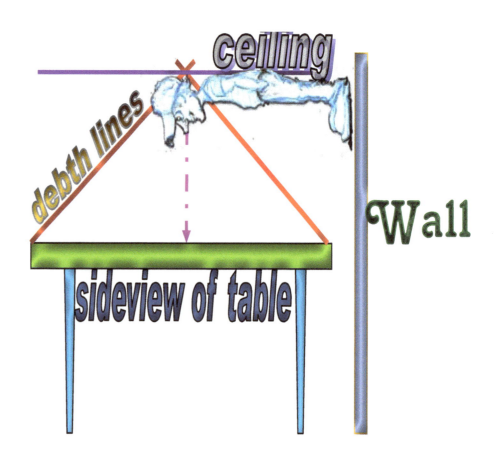

STEP 6
EYE LEVEL
FOR WORMS EYE

1. You are facing the short end of the table
2. Bend just a bit until you see JUST THE MIDDLE OF THE LEDGE of the table.
3. You will NOT SEE the TOP OR THE BOTTOM of the table.
4. The positions now are reversed, instead of rising to see the TOP of the table, you will be SQUATTING!

5. So you will follow the steps of the birds eye, but just reverse it until you get to the full worms eye then you will be lying directly under the table, and looking up as the next

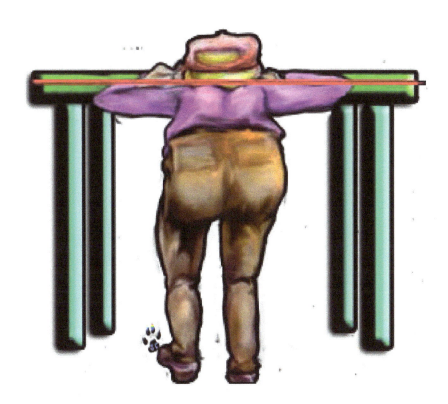

STEP 7
FULL WORMS EYE VIEW
(Which is the same as bird's eye
So this last step you are lying directly under the table where you see the full underneath of the table.

I think that you get the idea now
so let's get drawing and put these concepts in use!

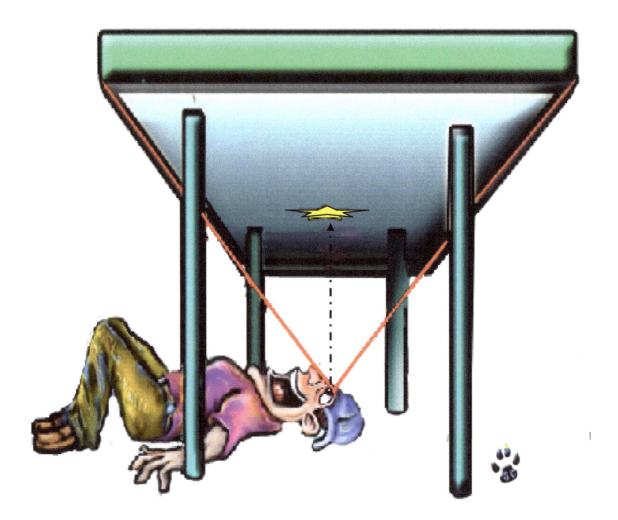

CHAPTER EIGHT
HORIZON LINE

First, I want to refresh your memory and reiterate again that this term "CAMERA VIEW" IS MY TERM which I use to help the artist to differentiate between a picture FROM A CAMERA that they are going to draw from, and drawing from a natural scene.

To elaborate a bit more, I use the term "CAMERA VIEW" to help the artist when they are using a PICTURE that you find in a magazine, book or on line.

But, it is also used in real life when YOU are using your OWN camera! OR... using your EYEBALLS!

When you are looking at a picture, the CAMERA VIEW is the simplest way to show you where the EYE LEVELS (BIRDS, WORMS and STRAIGHT ON EYE LEVEL) have been established and where and how the photographer is positioned in the picture.

The second reason I use the term "CAMERA VIEW" is to be a reference that will help the artist that wants to draw from REAL LIFE using their EYES as a camera

So, on the next pages I will now elaborate with illustrations just what I am trying to explain.

1. The CAMERA VIEW is where your position yourself when viewing the object. These positions come in 3 viewing levels… EYE LEVEL BIRDS EYE, OR WORMS EYE.

2. Your body position determines how much of the surface PLANE of the object you will be seeing.

3. The CAMERA VIEW is the first step you need to have in order to establish the HORIZON LINE and VANISHING POINTS

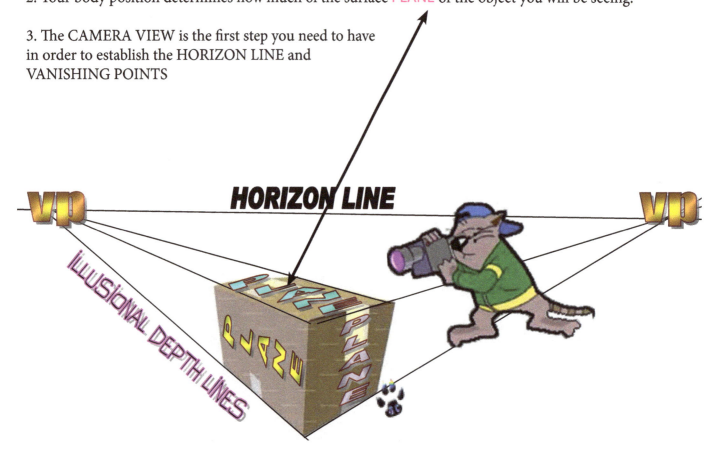

The horizon line has two sets of rules that you need to know.

THE FIRST SET OF RULES IS…
A.: **WHAT IT DOES**

B: **WHERE IT'S AT**

THE SECOND SET OF RULES IS:

C. **ARE YOU DRAWING FROM A PICTURE?**

D. **OR ARE YOU ESTABLISHING THE HORIZON LINE FROM A REAL SCENE?**

FIRST SET OF RULES EXPLANATION
A. "**WHAT IT DOES.**"

First of all, <u>MY</u> artistic definition of what a HORIZON LINE is:

It is Home Base for all vanishing points, **WHICH HAS BEEN CREATED BY THE DEPTH LINES COMING OFF OF THE OBJECT.**

What the Horizon line **DOES** is helps to accurately establish the sise of the plane of the object due to WHERE you are looking in other words, all of this depends on how high or low your position is when you are looking at this object.

The Horizon line keeps one from drawing inaccurately the size of the top or bottom planes. Meaning that if you see the top plan as a ½ view you **WILL NOT** draw it as a 1/8th or ¼ view throwing off your depth perpective on this object.

It is a guide line for you to use to be as accurate as possible.
The HORIZON LINE is **AUTOMATICALLY CREATED** when you draw the depth lines off of the object top and bottom edges and where they finally cross. (*THIS IS ESPECIALLY TRUE WHEN YOU ARE DRAWING FROM A PICTURE.*)

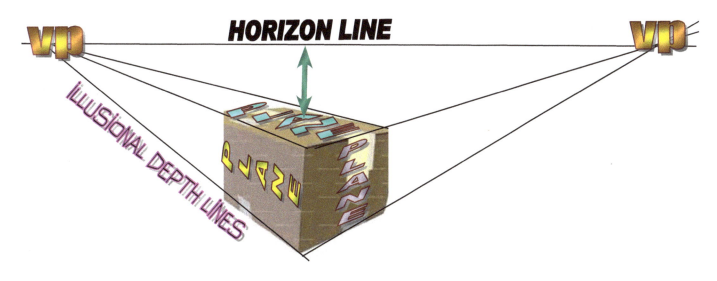

B. "WHERE IT'S AT"

The horizon line is found either at the TOP OF THE OBJECT which has been created by the depth lines if you are **<u>LOOKING</u>** at it at a BIRDS EYE.

Or the BOTTOM OF THE OBJECT that has been created by the depth lines if you are **<u>LOOKING</u>** at it from a WORMS EYE.

And if you are LOOKING AT THE OBJECT STRAIGHT ON, it is found in the MIDDLE of the object for there are no depth lines to be seen.

This is usually the most used method of drawing because there here are millions of wonderful shots in which to capture the imagination of an artist.

But this is where the problems really come to pass…

HOW TO MAKE THE DRAWING LOOK LIKE THE PHOTOGRAPH?

THE SECOND SET OF RULES

C. DRAWING FROM A PICTURE

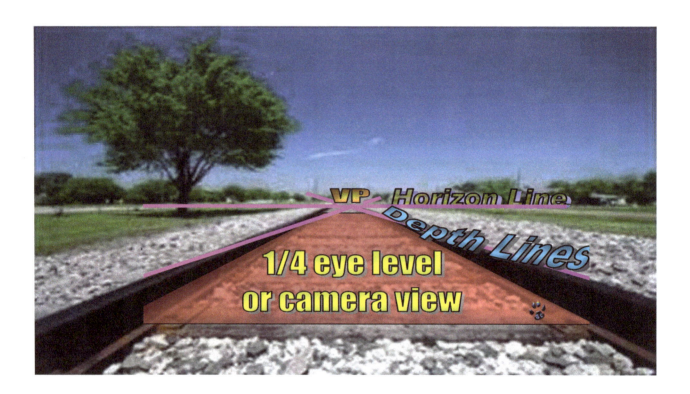

The photographer in the railroad picture on the opposite page must be lying on their stomach looking down the tracts to where the camera is focused on the distant trees. Their body would be half raised resting on her elbows in order to get this eye level,(or camera view.)

D. DRAWING FROM REAL LIFE USING JUST YOUR EYES.

Drawing the horizon line from real life is a bit more complex because this is now involving you getting a physical EYE LEVEL without a camera.

Meaning: Where are you conscientiously looking? Where and WHAT are your eyes physically focusing on?

So here are the steps you need to take in order to get the horizon line from real life. Remember, the VIEW of your object that you are looking at with your EYES will be affected by the physical posture you take. Such as lying flat on the floor, kneeling, sitting, crouching, standing, standing on a stool, ladder, or wall,

IN each position you choose to take you will:
1. LOOK STRAIGHT, AHEAD
2. The object that you focus on is now considered the HORIZON LINE.
3. Any 3-dimensional objects that are in front of the established HORIZON LINE can now be drawn accurately using the DEPTH LINES.
4. Remember, the DEPTH LINES have ORIGINATED FROM THE OBJECT that you are drawing!

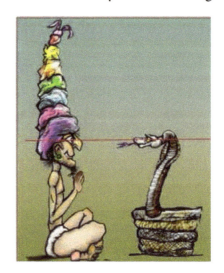

This view is EYE LEVEL WITH THE SNAKE AND MAN, because these two are on an equal eye level plane with one another. One is NOT higher or lower than the other as in the illustration of the man and the cat.

The drawing on the left is what she will see which is ¾ BIRDS EYE.

It's not a full birds eye because she is NOT directly over the top of him..but is sitting at a distance and her view is ALSO based on her height vs the height of the squirrel even though she is kneeling, she still towers over the squirrel.

The squirrel is looking directly at her stomach in this picture. He is about 4 feet away from her so it's her stomach that would be the most prominent view he'd see.

The squirrel, while looking at her stomach, he would see the top and bottom of her body would be a bit distorted and appear smaller because his peripheral vision can take in just so much undistorted information before his sight starts to disfigure what he is seeing. (This is what could be called a 'FISH-EYE' view.

I have given you a lot of information to try and digest, and I know that a 'pocket version' of trying to remember all of this would be nice, but impossible because of all the information that is needed to make a picture come out right.
But, mayhap this little nonsensical 'ditty' can be a fun way to remember what dimension is.

It's based off of the *'BONE CONNECTION SONG."*

"The hip bone is connected to the thigh bone, the thigh bone is connected to the leg bone, and the leg bone is connected to the foot bone…"
So…replace those words and now you will sing…

THE 3-DIMENSIONAL OBJECT is what you are focusing on with your EYES OR CAMERA

WHICH WILL BE <u>MANIPULATED</u> BY ....

"THE EYE (CAMERA) VIEW that will ESTABLISH the SIZE and DEGREE of the PLANES & ANGLE by WHERE YOU ARE LOOKING.

WHICH WILL <u>CREATE</u> THE...

THE DEBTH LINES that WILL BE RUNNING OFF OF the 3-DIMENTIONAL OBJECT

WHICH WILL <u>CREATE</u> THE...

THE VANISHING POINTS which have been **CREATED FROM** the DEPTH LINES that are RUNNING OFF of the 3-DIMENTIONAL OBJECT

WHICH WILL <u>ESTABLISH</u>...

THE HORIZON LINE that has been ESTABLISHED **BECAUSE** of the VANISHING POINTS.

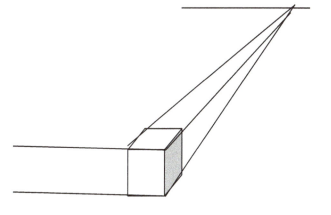

(WHAT 'POINT' IS THIS 3-D OBJECT? 1, OR 2 POINT?
AND WHAT FRACTION OF EYE LEVEL DO YOU SEE?)
ANSWER IS ON LAST PAGE OF THIS CHAPTER. (answer on next page.)

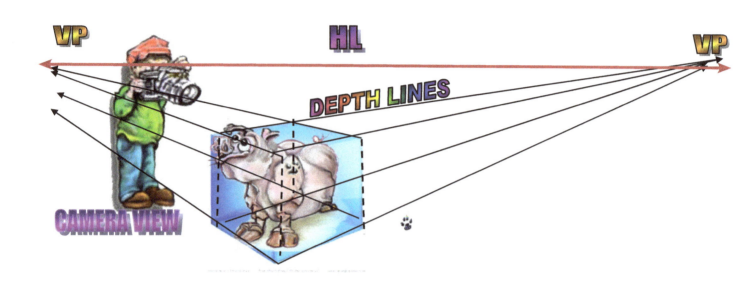

These depth lines will eventually cross but due to the restrictions of the size of the paper I cannot get the full distance it's going to take to get the LEFT VP crossed - Just know that they will cross where the green horizon line is

This is a two point 1'2 bird's eye view look at the size of the top plane on the blue box.

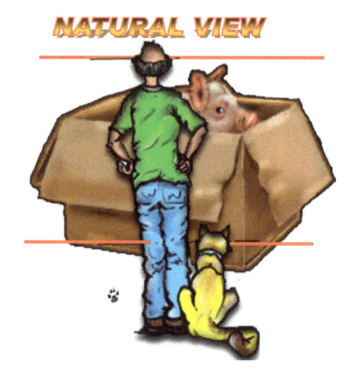

You will notice that I have really pounced on EYE LEVEL, CAMERA VIEW and how to get them. I have reiterated over and over the language and the actions that goes with this verbiage which is necessary to help cement these rules in your memory bank.

This part of learning art is always the hardest because it is the most confusing.
These rules are nigh on impossible to teach without becoming dry, boring, and confusing…and I had many a teacher when I was learning have a really difficult time getting the students to understand these rules.

They knew the rules, but couldn't explain them without sounding so technical that many a promising art student couldn't find the door fast enough screaming, **"FORGET THIS!, I'M 'OUTTA HERE !"**

BUT… once you understand this concept as well as apply what you have learned about the DIMENSIONAL RULES to the subject you want to draw, I feel that you will be successful in piecing together this first important step in drawing.

Now it is time to go onto the **THEORIES** of art in section two of this book.

This section will add the "REST OF THE STORY" to help you put the finishing pieces of this puzzle together, and help you become the successful artist I know you can be.

> answer to question
> *(IF YOU SAID 2 POINT… AND 1/2 CAMERA OR EYE LEVEL…
> YOU ARE CORRECT, CAN YOU EXPLAIN WHY?
> THIS IS TO TEST TO SEE IF YOU REALLY
> UNDERSTAND THE THEORIES OF THIS CHAPTER.)

Book Two
THEORIES

CHAPTER 9
INTRODUCTION TO THE 12 THEORIES

When I was teaching I noticed that there were certain problems that came up that confused the student even after they learned the basics.

The basics teach how and where to look at an object in the "skeletal form" of drawing.

Learning these basics is a major framework for drawing your picture accurately, but unfortunately the basics don't tell you how to finish off the rest of the "art house."

There is a lot more to drawing than just perspective understanding and this is where a lot of times the student isn't "filled in" on just how to make either their copied work or out of your imagination" pictures come alive.

And this is where the concept of my 'THEORIES' come in.

During the next 12 chapters I am going to attempt to complete the 'art house' that I started in section one in a fun and easy way.

THE SECOND SECTION OF THIS BOOK WILL
CONSIST OF 12 THEORIES

1. "THE PHYSICS OF "LUMPY AND BUMPY" theory…
Artistically understanding the surface PHYSICS of an object.

2. "YOU ARE NOW A MICROBE" TRAVELING OVER
'LUMPY AND BUMPY SURFACE" theory… Lessons of how
to mentally feel the surface of the object you are drawing,

3. "THE COFFEE CUP" AND HOW NOT TO LOOK LIKE
A GREEN HORN WHEN DRAWING THE OVAL" theory…
Mentally seeing and understanding the physics in something round or oval and applying it to a foreshortening problem.

4. "THE "SMILE & FROWN " theory… By looking at the outside curve of a circle or oval you will find it is a shortcut that helps you determine if the outside curve of an object is either in a SMILE or a FROWN. This will tell you what VIEW you are seeing the object at. (EYE LEVEL, BIRDS OR WORMS) and this will also enable you to estimate the amount of open space the top of the object has such as: 1/8, ¼, ½.

5 ."THE PROTRACTOR SPECULATION" theory …This is a 'shortcut' to look at the corner angles of a box or rectangle and using OR IMAGINING using a protractor to get the correct degree of these angles¾.5.

6 "THE "HAPPY "Y" & TIRED "T" theory… This is a short cut on finding an angle, and   degree of the angle on a box or rectangle that you see from a PICTURE. This helps you tell what depth the camera view is either from a birds eye ore worms eye view.

6.. "THE COIN" theory … Lessons for finding the middle line on anything which will help you find proper perspective in a turned object.

7. "THE GLASS GHOST" theory …Lessons in seeing through the object in order to draw everything in proportion, especially if the object is at angle.

8 "THE SPIDER-WEb" theory…Understanding how to look for negative shapes within the positive shapes to achieve accuracy when copying a picture.

9. " THE BUTTERFLY MORPHING" theory…Taking a stick drawing and making it into a manikin, then 'morphing ' your drawing into the correct proportional and perspective drawing.

11. "THE BUCKING BRONCO "theory…The study of movement in your drawings.

12. "WHY ARE YOU LOOKING AT YOUR THUMB?" theory…Lessons in sighting objects by using your thumb or pencil for drawing accurate real life objects.

CHAPTER 10
THE PHYSICS OF LUMPY AND BUMPY

Chapter Summary: Artistically understanding the PHYSICS of a living object which will start you on the road to making your picture come alive.

There are several ways of studying objects, but the three MAIN ways are:

        1. WITH PICTURES
        2. WITH REAL OBJECTS
        3. IN YOUR MIND

LET'S START WITH PICTURES

I like to start the student artist with pictures.

Pictures do not go anywhere and the student has time to study it without the time factor of a classroom, changing light sources or the object moving.

As you study and start to understand what you are looking for in a picture take that knowledge to a REALISTIC object.

To help you see what I am writing about let's take this picture of "**Mr. Puma.**"

This is just a nice picture of a black and white shot of a puma face, subtly shaded in warm and cool gray tones and tints with a splash of black and white for accent.

Looks pretty easy to copy right?

So you try a line drawing of the cat but it comes out looking FLAT with no life and a bit out of proportion.

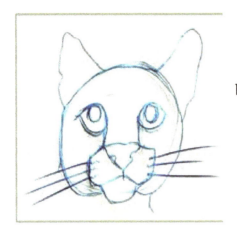

but you think it can be corrected by shading …

NOPE…it's seems pretty, but it still comes out flat…

Because this animal is REAL, this means that this animal has:

WEIGHT, MASS, & VOLUME

SO….WHAT'S THAT MEAN?

This animal has bone, muscle and blood vessels with flesh folding over its face and body like a pastry sheet over uncooked apples in an apple pie.

To help you visualize what I'm saying, I have made a series of 'blocks, angles, and steps' on this puma's face...these are the subtle results of:

WEIGHT, MASS, AND VOLUME

that is found on the anatomy of his face.

DEFINITIONS OF THESE TERMS

Volume: Bulk, Mass, Amount.
The amount of space occupied by a three-dimensional object

Weight: Heaviness, pressure, Mass, density, molecular substance.

MASS: A body of matter, heap, lump, bulk, piece, portion, bulk - pile -section of a body, or unit. A coherent, typically large body of matter with no definite shape. This leads us into the SECOND sub-sub-set of words explaining the physical properties of this puma's face.

PLANES
MOVEMENT
DIMENSIONAL SHAPES

DEFINITION OF PLANE, MENTAL
MOVEMENT, AND DIMENSIONAL SHAPE FOR THE ARTIST

The next pages will be explaining HOW you are to see real objects in your head when you see either REAL objects or PICTURES of a real object. By doing this your drawings then will start to come alive because you will be aware of the subtle hills and valleys of any surface. By understanding this therory you will be able to SHADE your pieces, either black or white or color with the knowlege of how light is effecting these hills and valleys.

You will then be able to understand how to BRING OUT the subtlenesses of the object you are drawing by being able to "SEE" these subtle hills and valleys...

Of course knowing the objects anatomy is really essential in UNDERSTANDING what muscle is where and how it affects the surface of a REAL LIVE SUBJECT such as this cougar. This will take practice to be able to be a SUPERMAN'/WOMAN to see below the skin and how the muscles are making the skin undulate.

PLANES: A flat; level or having to do with flat surfaces peaks and points and lines that have angles.
And when these flat and angled surfaces are put together in perspective they form 3-d shapes such as you see in this craggy mountain scene, and these boxes.

MENTAL MOVEMENT:

MENTAL MOVEMENT is when you feel the surface of your object with your eyes closed and mentally <u>***"SEE and FEEL"***</u> the undulating surfaces of the object you are trying to draw.

A good example is if you are riding a mental roller coaster.

RESULTS OF WHEN YOU DO THIS

DRAWING: When you draw your subject, you can mentally think of what direction the obvious and subtle 3-dimensional' hills and valleys' planes are going…up ,down, sideways, or around.

SHADING: When you can form a mental image of these planes, hills and valleys in your mind, you then will become aware of where the light source is coming from and how it is **AFFECTING** these physical bumps and lumps (also known as PHYSICS) in your subject.

By being aware of the lights PHYSICS on your subject and how it is affecting the subtle colors, tint's tones, light and darks of **EACH PHYSICAL PLANE** you will be able to shade it with knowledge of the **PHYSICS** of what the LIGHT is doing to your picture.

Then in the final stages of your drawing you will seamlessly blend in these subtle shades which will give you the effect of movement, reality, touchability, and believability to your drawings.

DIMENSIONAL SHAPES

The DIMENSIONAL SHAPES are physical forms that you see both subtlety and obviously, such as circles, triangles, box, ovals, and rectangles.

Now, when you add more DIMENSIONAL PLANES to these 2-DIMENSIONAL SHAPES, such as the BALL, TRIANGLE, BOX, RECTANGLE OVAL, you now will get your 3-DIMENSIONAL SHAPES such as: sphere (out of a ball) pyramids, (out of a triangle) cubes, (out of a box) cones, (out of a triangle) cube, (out of a box) cylindars (out of ovals) and rectangle (and for a rectangle, one can use the word 'brick' without getting geometrically fancy)
(REVIEW: 3- DIMENSION IS :HEIGHT, WIDTH AND DEPTH)

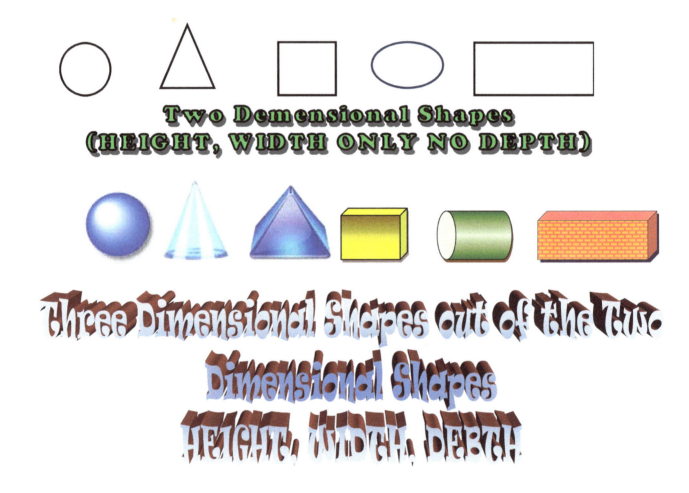

Two Demensional Shapes
(HEIGHT, WIDTH ONLY NO DEPTH)

Three Dimensional Shapes out of the Two Dimensional Shapes
HEIGHT, WIDTH, DEPTH

OK, SO WHAT DO THESE SHAPES MEAN FOR THE ARTIST?

Let's look at four examples of "Mr. Puma."

What do you see?

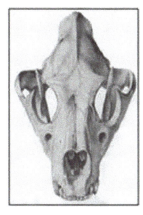   

1. A Skeleton (Figure A.)
2. The muscles of the face of the Puma (B)
3. The "Hills and Valleys" of the face (C)
4. The real puma (D)

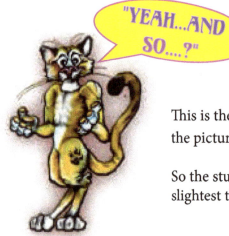

This is the main problem that most students have when they look at the picture and just see ONLY the **'REALISTIC PUMA.'**

So the student puts pencil to paper and tries to draw it without the slightest thought of this mountain lions anatomy.

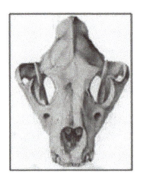

They do NOT THINK about the bony frame that give this lion head it's shape   (FIGURE A.)

And they really DON'T THINK about the muscle, fat, and bones that now have given the lion subtle hills and valleys when the skin is put over it. (FIGURE B.)

Because of the muscles and fat that has been molded over the bones of the lion, they cannot FEEL in their mind and fingers the rolling planes, hills and valleys that are the results of this undulating muscle and fat mass which is what will create MOVEMENT and the physical lumps and bumps CHARACTERISTICS of this animal. (FIGURE C)

Thus, when the student tries to draw the lion, it still comes out flat. But, then when these facts are pointed out and the student finally sees them, it is still hard for them to put the **PHYSICS** into the face!

They see a triangle or rectangle, but they see it as FLAT, 2-DIMENSIONAL shapes which is NOT something that has VOLUME, WEIGHT, and MASS! (They see a triangle, not a pyramid, or a square and not a cube, square, not a block, a circle, not a sphere.) Until this happens, any artistic rendering will always look flat …

So, how do you put
WEIGHT
MASS
VOLUME
PLANES
MOVEMENT-
DIMENSIONAL SHAPES
all together?

I've taken the real puma and planed it, so you can see the angles steps that subtly that are in his face.

Now, in the second picture I've done a quick job of shading which I've picked up some of the tones and tints of this animal but it's still flat.

To some eyes this rendering looks acceptable, but in a master's eyes, it's still flat and shows no movement no life…it's JUST an OK rendering.
la de da!

And sadly, this is what happens when the teaching of "movement" is NOT explained fully to the student. And this word is lost in the confusion of the other mass of weird words thrown at them in the hopeful expectation that eventually the student will pick up this concept by osmosis and through trial and error.

It's like playing music without the knowledge of what the notes mean and how they MAKE the music. They play by ear and the seat of their pants. The music is acceptable but not great!

Another confusing word is "FEEL" your picture.

And I KNOW through experience just how the student is scratching their head over this term. It means absolutely nothing to the student because in their mind how do you "FEEL" something that is on a 2-d piece of paper?

It is like shouting at a student that is trying to learn French and hoping through the shouting that the student will pick up the language.

And so like the fable of the "**KING'S NEW CLOTHES**" and not wanting to look like an incompetent boob, they pretend to understand, but the "proof is in the pudding'" when the drawings come out flat and lack emotion and movement.

Now, in the a quick sketch drawing of the third cat, I have enhanced in my shading to try and bring out the planes of the face that have been made by the interior muscle and bone structure of this animal. I know this animal's muscle and bone structure enough to draw what I really can't see in this picture. And I have quickly indicated the subtle hills and valleys that are needed to bring out the reality or realism of the puma.

I have taken liberties to exaggerate his face just a bit to make a point.
In conclusion, drawing without the proper study of anatomy really spells disaster and a flat piece of work. That is why, when I teach my students they are required to learn the anatomy of human and two animals of their choice.

They take each section of the body, such as the upper leg, draw the upper thigh bones, and then render a nice drawing of each layer of muscle that the upper thigh has. Then name each separate muscle and what they do.

I joke with them when I tell them by the time they finish my course, they could apply to become a veterinary assistant or a nurse's assistant, or become a physical or occupational therapist!

But, in the end my goal for the student is to become a competent artist. Then they can go out and know that what they draw, no matter what it is, will be alive, and an extension of what they feel and what they want to say.

The next chapter will be on "YOU ARE NOW A MICROBE" THEORY Which will further drive home this concept of movement, and how to mentally feel the surfaces of the object you're drawing.

CHAPTER 11
"YOU ARE NOW A MICROBE"
How to mentally feel the surfaces of the object you're drawing,

You are going to enter a realm of Sci-fi.

I want you to imagine that you are now going to be transported down into a very tiny microbe, where everything that you see is going to be bigger than the "grand canyon."

You are going to be entering a world similar to the wonderful movie of **"Honey I've Shrunk the Kids."**

Or you will be even smaller than the Alice of Lewis Carroll's 'Alice and Wonderland' where Alice is so tiny that even the caterpillar looks huge.

The first theory of lumps and bumps has brought out the knowledge that most everything in nature and manmade has hills and valleys, ups and downs, planes, and angles. (Discussed in chapter 10)

So, what I want you to do is take a little ride with me as a tiny microbe, where these hills and valleys, ups and downs, and angles now have become an adventure…a jungle of curves, and twists and turns, and roller coaster rides as you climb a hill and slide down the other side.

By doing this in your mind, you are now experiencing what is 'SEEING' AND FEELING the physical features of your subject.

This will force you now to REALLY, REALLY, REALLY look close at your subject.

Here are two examples that will help you see what you must do to help you mentally FEEL your piece so that you may sketch it then shade and color it with accuracy and 3-dimensional properties to your work.

First, here is an example of a boot (courtesy of Burne Hogarth's book, "Drawing Dynamic Wrinkles and Drapery.)

On top of the boot is
Humphrey the Microbe
"and those red lines is his travel path
up, down, around, in, and out of the wrinkles. So you see his journey which is fraught with hills and valleys he has to transverse.

Now pretend this subject is real, so. take your mental fingers and lightly touch these hills and valleys.

And when you are doing this, try to imagine yourself as a Humphrey and make your mind travel up, down, over, around, and across to become one with your fingertips.

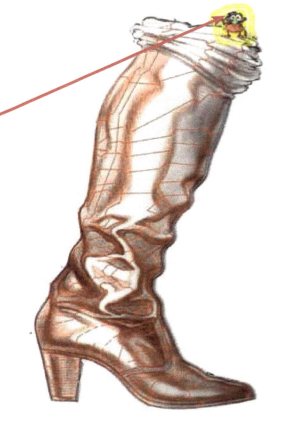

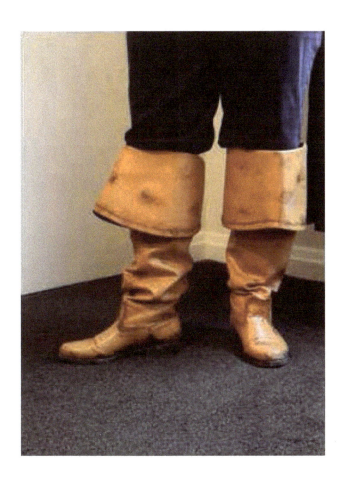

THEN DRAW WHAT YOU HAVE JUST EXPERIENCED!

Don't be afraid to constantly go over the surface with your fingers. This will create 'muscle memory' and eventually your brain will pick up and transfer what your fingers are feeling.

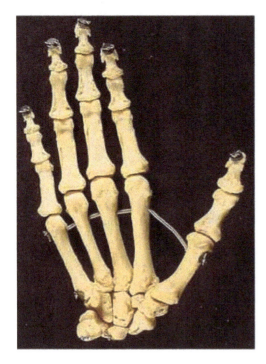

Now example two, if you are drawing from a PICTURE of an animal or human then start studying the anatomy.

See how the muscle reacts to the bone juts and then see how the skin folds over the joints and juts of hips, knuckles, backbones, kneecaps, ankles, etc. and don't just LOOK at the general curve of these sights, but become aware of the subtleties of what is not obvious.

For example, let's take the knuckle on the human hand.

Do you see in this picture the hills, valleys, curves and spaces?

Now take a look at your own hand.

Make a fist and REALLY LOOK AT YOUR KNUCKLE and see the two points of how the bone has made the skin undulate over those two bones?

Now become a microbe and travel over those two bones and slide down the ridge that leads onto the finger bone itself (the phalange).

Ok, now travel into the 'cavern' that is between those joints. Then feel with your other hand the space between those two joints.

This again is another version of 'FEELING' YOUR WORK WITH YOUR MINDS EYE…to really SEE your subject…and to understand it enough to be able to draw it with EMOTIONAL FEELING.

NEXT PAGE IS A SMALL LESSON IN LIGHT AND SHADING AND HOW THE UNDERSTANDING OF BEING A MICROBE WILL MAKE YOUR WORK COME OUT LIKE A MASTERS…

LIGHT EXPLANATION IN A NUTSHELL

The real simple explanation of light consists of "rods" and "cones."
i will deal with just 'rods.' from the sun or a light source.

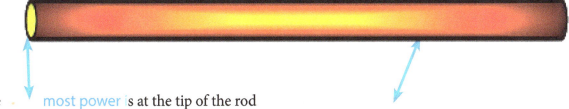

the   most power is at the tip of the rod
but on the sides of the 'rod' the light is diffused and weak
light 'rods' do not bend. they reflect but they will seem to curve when reflecting in water.

When looking at a curvy surface these curves consist of 'hills and valleys'
the lightest point of the surface is the top of the 'hill' as the 'hill' slips d into a valleys, the light then starts to

weaken and finally reach it's darkest point in the deepest recess's of these 'valleys until it reaces a flat surface even in a valley to receive the full benefit of the light..as you can see in the example above..again, this is because the rods' do not bend… this is called transitional gradation.. and will look like this:'
but once the tip of the light rods hit the hard surface of what the item is sitting on, it will reflect and bounce back illuminating the bottom edges of the item…as you see in this illustration.

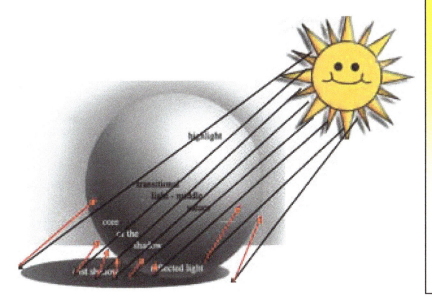

ANYTHING **THAT STICKS OUT** OF AN OBJECT WILL BE RECIPIENT OF THE MOST POWER OF LIGHT FROM A ROD. BOTH BY THE SIDES OF THE ROD AS WELL AS A DIRECT HIT FROM THE ROD. THE FARTHER AWAY THE RODS ARE FROM **THE SURFACES OF THE OBJECT THE MORE INEFFECTUAL IT IS TO THE SHADING OR REFLECTION OF THE OBJECTS SURFACE DUE TO THE WEAKNESS OF THE LIGHT COMING OFF OF THE SIDES OF THE RODS. IT'S THE RODS THAT HIT THE OBJECT AS WELL AS THE DISTANCE OF THE RODS FROM THE OBJECT THAT WILL DETERMINE THE STRENGTH OF THE DIFFUSED SHADING OF THAT OBJECT.**

Specular vs. Diffuse Reflection

- in accordance with the law of reflection. Once the angle is determined, such as level (horizontal) surfaces, vertical surfaces, angled surfaces, and curved surfaces as depicted in the diagram below. The rays will bounce off of these surfaces abd highlighting these surfaces accordingly to the distances and strength of the sides of the rods

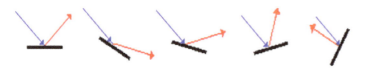

The Law of Reflection is Always Observed (regardless of the orientation of the surface)

Reflection off of smooth surfaces such as mirrors or a calm body of water leads to a type of reflection known as specular reflection. Reflection off of rough surfaces such as clothing, paper, and the asphalt roadway leads to a type of reflection known as diffuse reflection. Whether the surface is microscopically rough or smooth has a tremendous impact upon the reflections of a beam of light. The diagram below depicts two beams of light incident upon a rough and a smooth surface.

A light beam can be thought of as a bundle of individual light rays which are traveling parallel to each other. Each individual light ray of the bundle follows the law of reflection. If the bundle of light rays is incident upon a smooth surface, then the light rays reflect and remain concentrated in a bundle upon leaving the surface. On the other hand, if the surface is microscopically rough, the light rays will reflect and diffuse in many different directions.

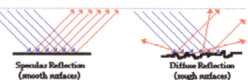

Why Does a Rough Surface Diffuses A Beam of Light?

For each type of reflection, each individual ray follows the law of reflection. However, the roughness of the material means that each individual ray meets a surface which has a different heights. The normal line at the point of impact is different for different rays. Subsequently, when the individual rays reflect off the rough surface according to the law of reflection, they scatter in different directions. The result is that the action of bouncing off any surface is determined by the surface of what it is hitting. The diagram below depicts this principle. Five incident rays (labeled A, B, C, D, and E) approach a surface.(REMEMBER LIGHT RODS DO NOT BEND!) The normal line (approximated) at each point of IMPACT is shown in black and labeled with an N. In each case, the law of reflection is followed, resulting in five reflected rays (labeled A,, B,, C,, D,, and E,).

Applications of Specular and Diffuse Reflection

There are several interesting applications of this distinction between specular and diffuse reflection. One application pertains to the relative difficulty of night driving on a wet asphalt roadway compared to a dry asphalt roadway. Most drivers are aware of the fact that driving at night on a wet roadway results in an annoying glare from oncoming headlights. The glare is the result of the specular reflection of the beam of light from an oncoming car. Normally a roadway would cause diffuse reflection due to its rough surface. But if the surface is wet, water can fill in the crevices and smooth out the surface. Rays of light from the beam of an oncoming car hit this smooth surface, undergo specular reflection and remain concentrated in a beam. The driver perceives an annoying glare caused by this concentrated beam of reflected light.

A dry asphalt roadway diffuses incident light.

When wet, water fills in the crevices, resulting in specular reflection and a glare.

This is Humphrey the elephant without the 'skin of shading, but he is showing the "skeleton" of how the artist should look at his lumpy and bumpy and hilly curves. and what is called the APEX's of all the MAJOR peaks of his anatomy, such as what you see here on his side, and on his trunk and knees and side of his legs. The apex of a major hill is a landmark to where it's going to be the lightest, to where the light rods hit the surface and get the full power of the illumination of the sides of the rods. Then as these rods go away from these peaks, the lighting will graduate in degrees of light to dark…

Humphrey now is showing a more 'mecahnical side of him, meaning taking the planes of what you see above and making these planes into 3-dimensional shapes… to maybe help show how the artist can see better how to shade the finished Humphrey even though you cannot see these hills and valleys in the drawing, but your inner eye can see them if you understand how ol' Humphrey is put together..

The final results of Humphrey the elephant due to the understanding of WHERE the hills and valleys and lumps and bumps are when looking at just an outline of him. You can see in your mind's eye the roundness of each wrinkle, and curve in his legs, trunks, side, cheek ears, knob on the top of his head, and his tail…

Remember…**The white areas are the furthest point that sticks out of the animal thus will get the most light**, as the protruding curves, the light will become gradually darker.

The outside of the elephant is lighter because of the reflected light bouncing off the floor back onto it's skin which is called REFLECTION.

CHAPTER 12
The COFFEE CUP THEORY and HOW NOT TO LOOK LIKE A GREEN HORN WHEN DRAWING THE OVAL

Chapter Summary: Understanding the physics of seeing the 3-DIMENSIONAL foreshortening in a circle or oval on a flat 2-DIMENSIONAL surface.

The most common question I am asked… "How do I make my superhero look like it's coming out of the page, and coming towards the reader?"

ANSWER: FORESHORTENING.

OK, WHAT IS THAT?

Well, I could just answer this question simply by saying in a dry fashion:

"Foreshortening is a technique used in perspective to create the illusion of an object receding strongly into the distance or background. Or coming out at you." (Google version)

OR another confusing version from the Google, Encyclopedia Britannica: "method of rendering a specific object or figure in a picture in depth. The artist records, in varying degrees, the distortion that is seen by the eye when an object or figure is viewed at a distance or at an unusual angle."

<u>Or, one can learn what my version</u> of what foreshortening is.

"FORESHORTENING IS AN ILLUSIONAL PERSPECTIVE TRICK THAT AN ARTIST USES TO GIVE THE IMPRESSION THAT THE CLOSEST OBJECT YOU SEE IS huge… WHILE THE REST OF THE OBJECT YOU'RE DRAWING will become very TINY AND moving back in BACKGROUND giving the viewer the feeling of depth.

So, you now are armed with several definitions you can choose from you now understand fully what foreshortening is and you can just draw up your comic book figure of

" Super-Dooper Princely Scooper" which will jump off the page and save the day …right?

No? You've tried and your figure STILL looks funny.

Ok, you are right, learning how to foreshorten is not that easy, and this has a lot to do with how you were taught to draw when you were just a kid scribbling outside the lines.
So, once again I am going to take you on a trip, but this time I'm going to take you back into your childhood when you were in:

where you learned these shapes,

Now you could start out your budding art career by building the traditional 2-DIMENSIONAL house with a smoking crooked chimney, one window with uneven lines, and an uneven path that went straight up in the air, one bulbous flower with five and a half-yellow petals, and explosion for a tree, with a mommy and daddy that was taller than the house, and a happy little sun, all squashed upon a hill.

Now time goes on and you are in fourth grade and you know that there is more to this **2-DIMENSIONAL** thing than a **CIRCLE, TRIANGLE, SQUARE, and RECTANGLE.**

Eventually you learn that these shapes in 3-DIMENSION now have a different name

CIRCLE= SPHERE or BALL

SQUARE=CUBE OR BOX

RECTANGLE or BRICK

TRIANGLE=PYRAMID

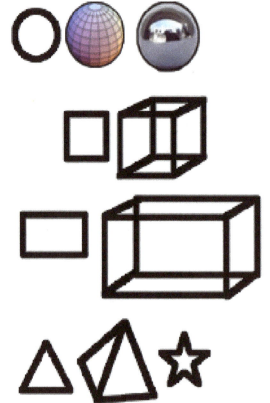

BUT!!!

It's the CIRCLE

that is going to become the
as you soon will see.

HERE'S WHY:

The circle is the only shape that one cannot draw lines to give it depth like you can with the box, pyramid, and rectangle, because you usually have to shade it in order to give it any sense of volume and form., or draw lines like you see in the illustration to the right.

But you are an artist trying to get the circle to have a solid look to on a 2-DIMENSIONAL piece of paper.

So a BALL which you are drawing as **JUST A LINE DRAWING** because you haven't SHADED it yet, and it is going to be seen as a ***FLAT 2-DIMENSIONAL CIRCL***E, even though your brain is saying: "BALL" or "SPHERE."

Now, it's not just the BALL that is difficult to define without any shading, but anything that has a a 3-DIMENSIONAL form to it that has a circle built-in to it, such as the top of a doughnut, dinner plate, a coffee cup, or a hamburger!.

Here are some examples to demonstrate my point: You will notice that most all of these pictures are a deep birds-eye view which does make a difference at this time.

Your brain interprets these round items as a circle because this is what you have been taught to do in spite of the fact that these are 3-DIMENSIONAL OBJECTS.

You see just the circle and this is easy enough because you don't have to draw the rest of the body that goes with these items.

But, a lot of the time you AREN'T going to be looking at items straight down because in order to make your picture more real you will be seeing them at a ¼, ½ or ¾ eyelevel or camera view.

And now you are faced with a different problem. This 'circle' has now become squashed and now it has become an OVAL.

OK, so it's now become an oval, but the problem is just the same as when you were looking at a circle.

BECAUSE….The circle and the oval both have:

So, once again one needs to understand the physics of the circle and oval in order to get your work to pop out at you, and look like it is 'touchable!"

Ok, let me go over the PHYSICS of these little nightmares.

There will be two steps:

1. The 'anatomy' of the circle which I will call The **"COFFEE CUP' THEORY."**

2. and, **"HOW NOT TO LOOK LIKE A GREENHORN WHEN DRAWING THE OVAL"**

"THE COFFEE CUP THEORY"
Understanding the anatomy of a circle

When I first started to teach I was faced with the students not understanding how to get things to come forward and look real. I saw that most everything they drew was flat, stiff and up in the air.

It was by accident that I happened to see out the corner of my eye the construction of a coffee cup. It struck me that the students could understand seeing the SIDE VIEW of it and how it STUCK OUT, but not "see" the physics of the FRONT of it until it was pointed out.

The students problem was:

"DRAWING WHAT YOU SEE! AND NOT WHAT YOU KNOW!"

This was the worm in the apple.

It was a young student that helped to put things in working words, so, I have honored him by calling this theory: "Tyler's Diamond Theory."

In order to get the students to understand how to visualize the concept of the direction of "OUT" or what I call, "IN YOUR FACE," I had the students draw a flat **2-DIMENSIONAL (H, W)** circle which represents a FULL BIRDS EYE VIEW of looking down into the coffee cup.

Then I ask them to draw a diamond where all four corners are touchin the north, south, east and west of
the cup like this:

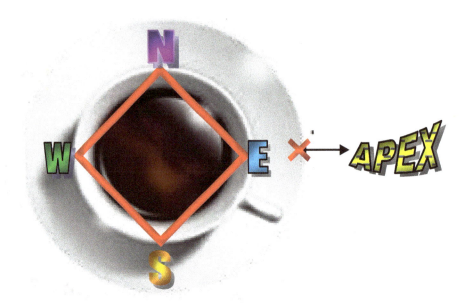

By doing this they were now able to wrap their brain around some sort of boundaries of this circle.

These "boundaries" are what is known as APEXES. They are the furthest outward bulge of a curve which is in the exact middle of the curve. Just before it starts in another direction,

YES, I know what is about to be said, "But this coffee cup has apexes all around because there is no stopping point," which is true.

But, then I asked the student, "So, how can it be determined where the front of the coffee cup starts. And how can one make sense of a beginning or end of a circle? Especially if they are drawing a glass, or round objects that don't have a handle?"

The answer is: *"THERE HAS TO BE A STARTING POINT SOMEWHERE* in order to draw the circle in a correct perspective dimension.

So, this is why and where the diamond shape helps set the boundaries of this cup in order to understand the concept of the "FRONT EDGE."

By putting the diamond in the center of the coffee cup, the points of the diamond now has established some boundary lines here to where there is going be some sort of direction.

It doesn't matter really where you turn the glass or cup without a handle or a round jar that has no marks on it to indicate where to start. For it will be all the same in the end. The diamond is just to help your eye and brain construct the PHYSICS of this eternal circle, and help you with physical outward landmarks.

"But," I had one student ask me, "If I look at a real glass at a straight on eyelevel all I see is a straight line. And this is also the same principal when I look at a eyelevel picture. So, there isn't any 'IN YOUR FACE" physics to speak of.

I then tell them that this is very true, but in real life this 'straight on line" is an illusion and that in real life it is pooching OUT, and to KNOW this because even though the top line of this glass or cup is straight the REST OF THE OBJECT IS NOT static and straight and flat!!!
.
This is where the mind has to go in order to make the object come alive. The FRONT of the glass is

coming OUT at you because the BOTTOM line of the glass is ROUNDED which will tell you that the physics of this glass just doesn't stop at the top or is ruled by what you see on the top when you are viewing it at this EYE LEVEL!

This is where it is VERY important to understand in their MIND HOW the object REALLY LOOKS in all views.

In other words their mind has to become sort of like an animators screen where they can twist and turn the object they are drawing in all different directions so that they can fully get the picture of the physics of this object.

Near-optimal Character Animation with Continuous ControlTreuille, A. Lee, Y. Popović, Z

Then when that happens,
they truly will start to understand how to look at ANYTHING with an educated eye that nothing that is 3-D is flat…when one's eye level is straight on.

There is another way this front edge can be called which will be the "southern edge." This is also the edge that will be IN YOUR FACE! This term means that this will be the closest thing to the viewer, and the first thing that is going to be seen as an illusion of it is "coming out at you" and BIGGER in size.

These three cups have some of the top showing in various different eye levels.
One can see how the diamond in these cups is affected as they become more 'squashed' as eye level (or camera view) is changing.

But the problem is: "HOW TO DRAW" these views and make them look like they are round without shading them?

The answer is in the forth cup, "The Problem Child." This little dandy holds the 'secret' in REALLY understanding this dilemma.

In this black cup all that is being seen is a straight line both top and bottom of the cup, because it is a straight on view or EYE LEVEL thus making this cup look 2-DIMENSIONAL-no debth to it. Height, and width only.

So it is being drawn as it is seen… la- de- da. FLAT!

Obviously again, the physics of this cup is NOT being thought about…

meaning how is this cup *REALLY SHAPED?*

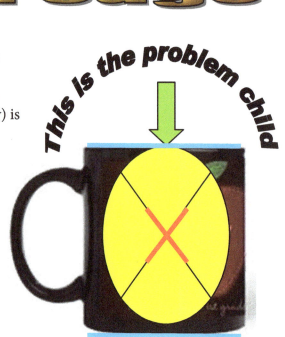

THE ANSWER IS: That it is THE MIDDLE of the cup that is the part that is coming **OUT AT YOU**, which means:

IT EFFECTS THE
TOP AND BOTTOM CORNERS OF THE CUP.

On the samples of the A & B cup below...The top of the cup looks to be straight, but it's the BOTTOM CURVE of this "A" cup that is 'smiling' indicating that this cup is CURVED! and not flat! (This theory will be covered in the next chapter the "Smile and Frown").

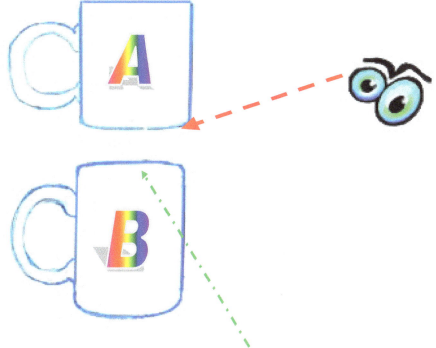

Now, take a look at the top of the "B" cup. It is in a versoft 'FROWN' which helps to give the illusion of some sort of 'movement' and makes the viewer know that this cup has some volume to it. (Also being as this curve is in a 'frown' it means that the camera view is LOOKING SLIGHTLY UP at the cup...BUT ONLY SLIGHTLY!!!!

Ok…this is fine and dandy, but the question is how is this going to make the cup seem more curvilinear when it's drawn straight on (or eye level) without the benefit of shading?

THE ANSWER IS:

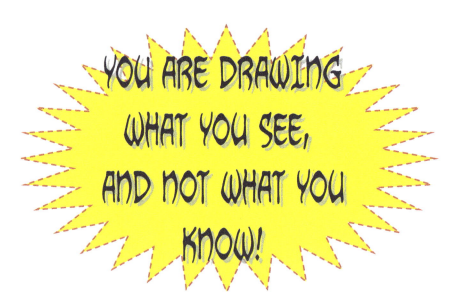

YOU ARE DRAWING WHAT YOU SEE, AND NOT WHAT YOU KNOW!

ONE KNOWS that the cup is a cylinder shape, but the EYES are saying that the cup looks 2-DIMENSIONAL and FLAT because one is looking at the cup at a straight on (EYE LEVEL) view. where the top and bottom lines looks perfectly STRAIGHT!

ONE KNOWS that the object that is being drawn is 3-DIMENSIONAL.

But the dilemma is: *"how do you draw this and make the drawing look believable when it is being rendered as just a LINE DRAWING?" (no shading)*

NOW THIS IS WHY ONE HAS TO BECOME AWARE OF THE DIAMOND THEORY

because it is necessary to keep in mind that in reality this cup is

POOCHING OUT

Unfortunately, in most cases this theory won't register in the brain for awhile unless it is consciously glued into the brain the

PHYSICS of this cup.

Take a look at this PICTURE of the cup on the right.

There is just a straight line on top of the cup that has a 90 degree, sharp right angle in a four of the corners, right?

BUT!!!! There is a solution to help soften the top lines of this cup.

This is where most students will fall flat on their face, because they are COPYING what they SEE but NOT what they KNOW!

They are seeing in this PICTURE of this cup, the HARD 90 DEGREE ANGLES. OF BOTH TOP AND BOTTOM CORNERS
(Even though the bottom of this cup does have a slight softening of the right hand bottom curve,)the overall portrait of this cup is hard and angled.

But IN REALITY the corners of BOTH top and bottom of the cup is NOT a HARD square 90 degree angle because the cup is ROUND and the corners of this cup, in real life, goes into a *softer curve* to give it the illusion of it curving AROUND .

But most of the time I see a student draw a glass or cup with this sharp corner, and this is what I call....

THE "EEERP STOP!" SYNDROME,

This is what has to constantly have to be kept in mind when one is drawing anything that has corners.

THESE CORNERS NEED TO BE ROUNDED! such as glasses, cups, bowls, and flower vases, etc.

One has to relentlessly be aware of WHERE and HOW they are looking at this object, and ask the question: "Is it EYE LEVEL, BIRDS EYE, OR WORMS EYE?"

SO AS A REMINDER, TRY to remember that if drawing from a picture, the camera only captures what the lens sees, it doesn't have a brain, and a lot of times when the camera is focused on an EYE LEVEL or ¼ EYE LEVEL such as this white cup… Its lens only sees the semi-sharp or sharp 90 degree lines that is depicted on it's corners that is circled in red.

It's these hazards that make this cup look flat. This is where one

SHOULDN'T DRAW WHAT YOU SEE, but DRAW WHAT YOU KNOW!!!

TO REVIEW THE PHYSICS OF A CIRCLE:

1. The circle when drawn just as a line drawing (no shading) looks flat or 2-DIMENSIONAL when looking DOWN upon it at a full BIRDS EYE.

2. To put the PHYSICS into the circle, draw a diamond to where all points neatly fit into the circle. This gives the circle boundaries

3. The points of the diamond are called "APEXES," which are the furthest bulge that is found in a curve

4. When viewing an EYE LEVEL cup (or looking at it straight on where you don't see the top or bottom) you will be seeing a straight top line and a small 'smile' on the bottom

5. Remember that the difference of looking and drawing from a PICTURE vs. REAL LIFE! In this EYE LEVEL This means you need to:

6. DRAW WHAT YOU KNOW…NOT WHAT YOU SEE!

7. Watch for the "EEERP STOP "sharp corners and round them to give the illusion of the object (cup in this instance) has volume

8. Round these corners slightly AND curve the top into a real small frown, And round the bottom into a slight 'smile' to give it 'movement 'and volume which will give it an illusion of, being 3-dimensional.

NOW ONTO THE OVAL

This little nightmare will **FORCE** you to become an artist, because it will mark you as an amateur if you don't conquer this form.

It is a slippery deceptive shape that puts all of us in our place for it is the hardest to conquer. The lines can slip and slide in the tiniest degree and when that happens, it throws off the whole shape!

The ends usually are squashed, uneven, pointy, lumpy, looking like a football, and curved in all manner of being totally wrong!

The sad thing about the oval is that MOST everything that contains a cylinder form will have this challenge , and when the camera is looking at it in various different heights, the tops of the cylinder will change in size and depth, which affects the rest of the picture. (EXAMPLE: A coffee cup and saucer.)

You draw the shape and it looks like semi- deflated football, with one side fat and the other side skinny which makes you sputtering angrily and wanting to throw your pencil across the room cause you have just gone though a half a sketchbook trying to fix what you have NO CLUE on how to.

But all's not lost and once you understand the PHYSICS of it, it's pretty simp

HERE'S HOW...

REMEMBER THE **APEX ?**

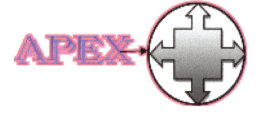

IT IS THE HIGHEST POINT *of a circle or curve before it changes directions.*

REMEMBER on page 104 where I pointed out In the circle **"Tyler's Diamond Theory"** where I put a diamond in the circle and labeled them: North, South, East, and West?

Ok. The circle is equal all the way around, meaning, no squashed edges.

THE OVAL IS NOT SO NICE…

For it's these 'squashed' edges that will drive a beginning artist nuts. These apexes are the areas to watch for, because they are the zones that slip and slide.

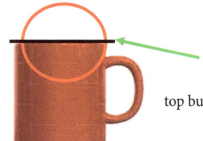

REMEMBER that the straight line is caused by viewing the cup at 'EYE LEVEL,' where you do not see ANY top but a straight-line.

THE NEXT FEW PAGES WILL SHOW EXAMPLES THE 6 CAMERA "EYE LEVELS" OF THE OVAL

I will put the width of the top in percentages:

STRAIGHT LINE ,1/8, ¼, ½, ¾ & FULL CIRCLE

the rabbit cup is an 1/8th eyelevel view see how narrow the top is? And see how 'squashed the edges are?
The camera angle is low and is aimed just above the edge of the cup.

These cups are considered a 1/4 opening because the 'surface is getting wider, showing more opening. And the APEX CURVES (marked by the "X") are getting wider exposing more of the surface or PLANE of the cup, because the camara view is moving slightly higher exposing more of the SURFACE OR PLANE of the cup.

THE ½ VIEW… the west and east edges are significantly rounder. And the opening is getting rounder. This is because the angle of the camera view is steadily climbing higher, exposing more surface of the cup. The circle of the cup is becoming rounder; the edges are not sharp as the 1/8 and ¼.

This is a ¾ view, notice that the camera view is quite high and the angle of your eyes now are looking ALMOST directly into the center of the cup.(In these two pictures the camera angle is at slightly different heights and because of this there is a subtle difference, but if you study these two ovals you will see that the coffee cup with the beans is slightly less round than the swirling coffee cup.

This is a **FULL BIRDS EYE** or a complete circle because you are looking DOWN fully into the cup. The camera view is looking directly over the top of the cup.

THE PROBLEM OVALS ARE USUALLY THE 1/8, 1/4, &1/2 VIEW

The 1/8th and the 1/4th cups are usually going to cause the MOST trouble for beginning artists. That's because in these two pictures, the eye is seeing that the WEST AND EAST edges are rather sharp and narrow.

Drawing them without making them look uneven is going to be difficult.
So, I know from experience watching the struggling attempt of my students this is what I usually get from them:

The worst area that slips and slide is the back half of the curve and one edge ok the other off.

Because most artists try and get the edges of the back half of the cup to line up with the front half.

This won't work because the front half of the cup has been ignored so they try and draw the back half higher in order to match up with the curvilinear 'smile' of the front half, making the cup look like it's going up in the air like I've demonstrated on the bottom cup.

The oval has the same rules as the circle.

It's the FRONT OF THE CUP that comes out.

BUT THERE IS A SLIGHT PROBLEM...

THE WEST AND EAST edges of the cup that causes the unevenness and the football pinching.

This iThis happens when the beginning artist is looking at the oval; they are drawing again what they see which is a 'foot ball' looking shape no matter at what camera view or eye level you are looking at.

But, when one starts raising their body over the cup or object (BIRDS EYE) they will start to notice that the curves on the west and east end will become wider. But, this still is going to pose as a problem when the cup or oval object is being drawn.

This is because the beginner will compensate these wider curves by still trying to draw the BACK PART of the cup to match up with the front of the cup. This is because the eye is lying, and is tricking the brain into making the hand try to balance the roundness of the cup by trying to match the back curve with the front curve.

Unfortunately, all this is doing, is making the oval go straight up in the air.

(IT ALSO HELPS IF THE VERTICAL LINES ARE STRAIGHT AND NOT LEANING HITHER AND YON!)

Now, I know that one has been taught that **CHEATING** is not good. But this is one of the only times that cheating is perfectly ok because the "IDEA" is to fool the viewers into seeing a realistic 3-DIMENSIONAL object.

And when drawing ovals and circles, one needs to **CHEAT.**

HERE'S HOW...

It's the FRONT END of the oval that needs to come out...NOT the back end.

It's important to keep the flatness of the oval.

And it's the FRONT END meeting up with the back line that is going to do that.

By PULLING OUT THE FRONT LINE, AND WIDEN THE WEST AND EAST CURVES this FORCES the OVAL TO STAY FLAT & STOP IT From going up in the air.

It's only when you do this will the oval cooperate and take on equal shape.

(Don't forget to round the bottom corners to avoid the "EEERP STOP!" effect.)

There is one more point that can come up....ok, this is fine for a ½ or a ¾ view, but what happens when one is faced with a 1/8 view or ¼ view? Where the oval is more 'squashed?'

How can 'foot-balling' the corners of the oval be avoided?

CHEAT!!!

Just because the eye is saying that the object that is being looked at seems to have pointed edges.

REMEMBER THE RULE:

Just widen the corners a bit more and bring out the front end of the cup just a pinch.

But I will be honest here. On the 1/8 eye level view it will be very hard NOT to have the cup look pinched because of the narrowest width of the top of the cup.

Due to the narrowness of the surface one will not be able to avoid the pinched look unless they 'cheat' a bit by pulling out the front line a bit more. It still will give you the effect of it being almost a 1/8 eyelevel, but this is a judgment call with the artist. (I do it because it makes the piece more believable and dimensional.) To repeat the drawing of the oval success for 'ol time's sake, remember:

It is important NOT to pinch these corners! **KEEP IN MIND TO BRING THE FRONT OF THE CURVE OUT.** It is a foreshortening example. And it means that the front of this curve will give the illusion that it is BIGGER!
 LEAVE THE BACK OF THE CURVE ALONE. The front of the curve is the "working" edge The west and east curves can be adjusted as the front curve is being pulled OUT.

It is important to determine the camera view, which will determine the horizon line

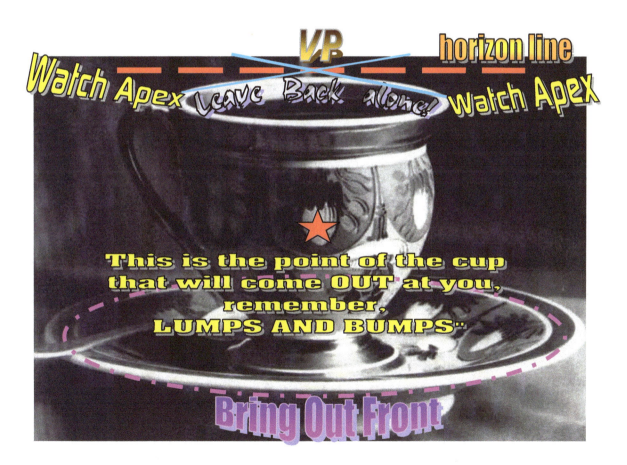

Now onto the "SMILE AND FROWN" theory which is a short cut on how to look at the edge of something round or oval from a picture, and tell what depth the EYE LEVEL (or camera view) is and if you are looking at the object at an eye level, birds eye, or worms eye.

CHAPTER 13
THE SMILE AND FROWN THEORY

This is a 'shortcut' on how to look at the edge of something round or oval from a picture, and tell what depth the camera view is, either from a BIRDS EYE OR WORMS EYE view. This is an extension of the 'Coffee Cup' theory.

This theory can be complicated because it is a perspective problem which involvs looking at an object in a manner of large to small, up and down, near and far.

And all of this is determined by where your camera is located. (BIRD'S EYE, EYE LEVEL, OR WORMS EYE and at what degree? 1/8th, 1/4th. ½ or 3/4ths).

This theory also involves how to accurately draw two or more objects and how the perspective of these items will be affected by the the circular depth (are they deep or shallow curved?) of the "smiles and frowns."

This theory also involves the accurate way to interpret the curvilinear lines that will help determine the correct angle of the curve, (the smile or frown) such as drawing the bottom of a shirt sleeve, or neck or bottom of the shirt.

By knowing the 'smile and frown' of the curve you then can judge the camera angle and view of the photographer, be it eye level, birds eye or worms eye.

These curves are also another clue on how the object flows around another object, such as this shirt which is being dictated by this person's body.

By also being aware of the direction of these curves this will prevent an inaccurate curvilinear movement making your picture look off and perspectivly flat.

OK… a few rules to follow

1. The curvilinear lines are going to be most affected by either looking UP OR DOWN at the object.. The HIGHER the horizon line **THE MORE** of the object 's bottom you will see. This means that the 'SMILE' of the **FRONT PART** of the oval (what I call a 'CUTE SMILE' is usually matched by an equally 'SOUR' FROWN IN THE BACK.

This will give the impression that you are looking **DOWN** and **INTO** the object.

2. The **LOWER THE HORIZON LINE IS, (OR AS THE CAMERAPERSON IS STOOPING TO GET THE SHOT)** the less you see of THE SURFACE (IN BLUE) This means that the curvilinear 'SMILE' is **BECOMING WIDER** and is matched by an **EQUALLY WIDER** frown, which means that your view of the inside of the object is getting harder to see amd it is obvious that the object is being turned.

So, to review this again, if you are looking DOWN at the object (**at an ¾ or** almost a **FULL BIRDS EYE**) you will notice that the front curvilinear line that you see, will be not as wide a 'smile', but a slightly more 'pinched' or 'U' shape giving you the illusion that you are looking down ,into the cup.

The 'frown' on the **BACK** of the cup will match the curve of the 'smile' in the **FRONT** of the cup. *REMEMBER: It's the edges you have to watch, and make them meet with an equal curve.*

3. If the camera is looking at the cup in a 1/4th, or 1/8th or ½ view then you will see that the smile on the cup is WIDER . (which means the TOP surface of the cups (in BLUE) are getting narrower) it is the same for the back of the cup, the 'frown.' This will start to give the illusion of the cup 'going back' depth.

4. The curvilinear lines (smiles or frowns) are going to be affected by how many objects are in the picture and where they are placed.

Such as, what objevts are coming AT you or GOING away from you? Or are they in a straight line, or staggered?

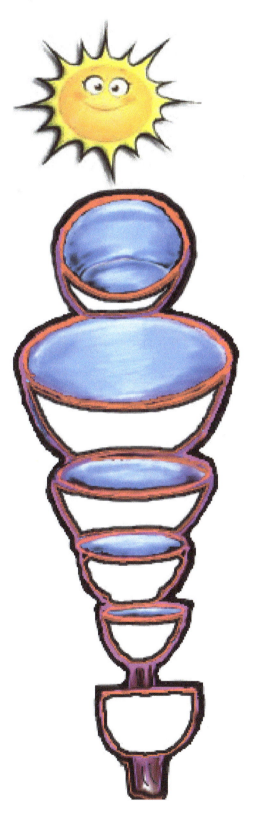

And where is the camera person taking the picture? (BIRDS EYE, EYE LEVEL OR WORMS EYE) and at what degrees are these eye levels at ,meaning is the camera positioned at a 1/8, 1/4,1/2 ,3/4. FULL? BIRD'S EYE OR FULL WORMS EYE view?)

REMEBER!!!!

THE HIGHER THE HORIZON LINE THE MORE PLANE YOU SEE.

THIS MEANS :

that the 'SMILE' of the oval is starting to become 'cuter' (or more "U'd) and is usually matched by an equally deep 'sour' FROWN in the back.

This will give the impression that you are LOOKING DOWN, into the object

So, in the soda pop picture the camera person is semi- crouched over these glasses aiming the camera about two to three inches ABOVE the glasses to where the planes of the ovals at a ½ view…. *(MEANING THAT THE HORIZON LINE IS ABOUT TWO AND A HALF TO THREE INCHES ABOVE THE GLASSES.)*

1. "The second thing you will notice is that the FARTHEST GLASS IN THE BACK, the 'SMILE' is not as tight, IT IS WIDER because it is FARTHER AWAY From the camera lens, and CLOSER TO THE HORIZON LINE because the glass is going away from your view and you are seeing less of the top plane .

The front two glasses are **"IN YOUR FACE!"** and the front and back curvilinear lines of these two glasses will become progressively more 'cute' and 'sour' as you position your body more OVER glasses, and you see more top plane.

I say **"PROGRESSIVLY"** because of the staggered position these glasses are placed. You will notice that the first glass which is closer to the camera, the edge of the glass is slightly more **SMILEY 'CUTE' (OR "'U"d)** and **FROWNING 'SOUR'** than the second glass which is behind it.

This is also going to give you the clue of your eye levels (which is birds eye)from a ½ view of the first glass, to a very small difference of ½ view of the second glass. Which is now SLIGHTLY further away from the camera view.

REMEMBER:. BIG TO SMALL!' & 'WIDE TO TIGHT' is a good way to remember how the perspective illusion of anything oval or round will give a 3-DIMENSIONAL illusion. (H.W,D.)

Now, here is where you will be drawing NOT WHAT YOU SEE BUT WHAT YOU KNOW …and this is where you can do a bit of *'CHEATING'* in order to make this CAMERA PICTURE illusionary correct on this TWO DIMENSIONAL sheet of paper. (H. & W.)

To take a closer look at this picture, you will notice that in the first two front glasses the ovals look almost the same right?

IN THE PICTURE they do look like that…but now knowing the rules of "IN YOUR FACE" means BIG, to small.

And knowing this, you can 'cheat' by adjusting slightly the second glass oval to where there is an bit of an obvious difference of size from the front glass. (But, don't go overboard!) because then you will have to adjust the third glass oval's smile and frown a bit too much in order to show a progression of oval size differences in order to show depth and this could make the picture come out too unbalanced and awkward.

Now I know what you are thinking… "Then,what you have written is a bit obvious being as these soda glasses are tapered."

Ok, so let's look at some regular glasses.

You can see the obvious oval difference in these brown glasses..

The first glass is an excellent example of a ¼ **plus degree** view and how the FRONT EDGE IS "IN YOUR FACE!"

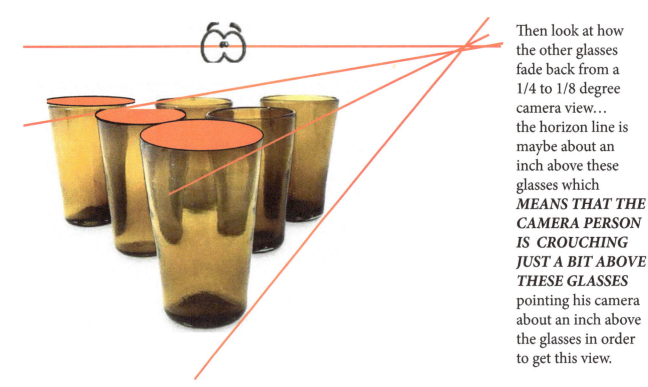

Then look at how the other glasses fade back from a 1/4 to 1/8 degree camera view… the horizon line is maybe about an inch above these glasses which **MEANS THAT THE CAMERA PERSON IS CROUCHING JUST A BIT ABOVE THESE GLASSES** pointing his camera about an inch above the glasses in order to get this view.

Now look at the 'smiles and frowns' of these glasses… notice at first glance, that the view SEEMS as though all of these glasses are the same?

Well, again in this picture, it's the camera illusion that has made this view look like this.

BUT…what's the rule? "DRAW WHAT YOU KNOW…NOT WHAT YOU SEE!"

You know the rule of "IN YOUR FACE" and that the curve of the very front glass seems to become BIGGER, because it is coming out AT YOU.

The front glass, being closer to the camera, the oval is going to be "smiley cuter", because you are looking DOWN MORE into the glass, thus the curve of the front smile is going to be slightly 'cuter'

Notice now, as they go back their 'frown' shape also will become more 'SQUASHED' AND WIDER because as they GO BACK .

The **TOP OVAL** PLANE (IN RED) is becoming SMALLER which will give the illusion of distance on this two dimensional piece of paper. (H.W.)

The front glass, being closer to the camera, the oval is going to be "smiley cuter", because you are looking DOWN MORE into the glass, thus the curve of the front smile is going to be slightly 'cuter' (or more "U'd") Notice now, as they go back their 'frown' shape also will become more 'squashed' and wider because as they go back the top oval plane is becoming smaller which will give the illusion of distance on this two dimensional piece of paper. (H.W.)

REMEMBER:

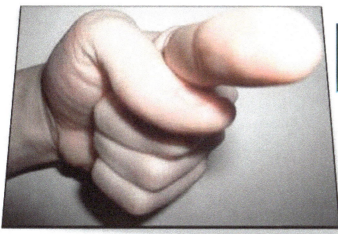

BIG TO small

Ok, one more example here so you can get a good idea of what happens in different views.

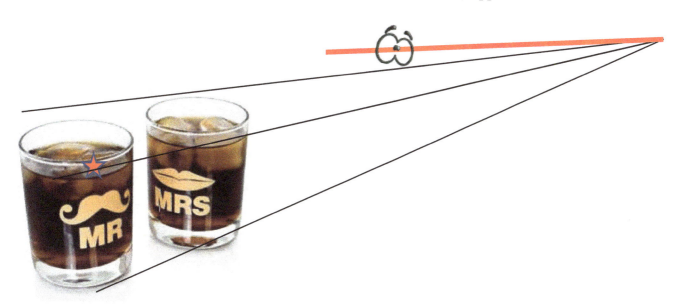

In this picture, the camera person has aimed the camera higher than they did on the brown glasses giving you a larger top plane view of the ovals.

At first glance again the glasses look the same don't they?

But they are not. There is a **_SLIGHT_** difference. Look at the front glass whhich is a bit closer and notice how it is "IN YOUR FACE?" *(see the star?)* just slightly more than the second glass?

This means again that you will have to draw "WHAT YOU KNOW, AND NOT WHAT YOU SEE." And CHEAT A BIT.

You will have to draw the smile of the front glass SLIGHTLY "CUTER", or (more "U" shape to give the illusion of it coming out at you, and give the viewer the illusion of looking down into the glass JUST A BIT MORE!

Do not over exaggerate it, for it will throw off the second glass and the perspective of both glasses. Which means that you will have to draw the second glass's smile just a BIT WIDER in order to give it the illusion that it is going away from you.

Now for the smile and frowns on a subject that can easily be drawn backwards, or having the curve the going the wrong way. On the following page you will see four shots of a manikin.

Here is an example of STRAIGHT ON VIEW there is NO curves anywhere..

BUT…here is a trick question..to see if you can put in practice the theory of DRAWING WHAT YOU KNOW-NOT WHAT YOU SEE!

In this picture there there is a slight FROWN curve…

CAN YOU SPOT which one it is?

ANSWER AT END OF CHAPTER.

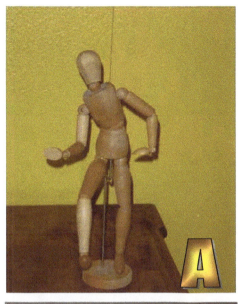
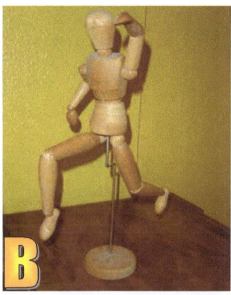
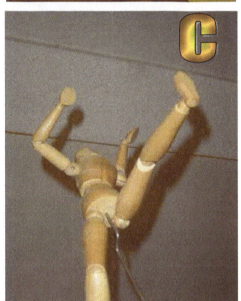
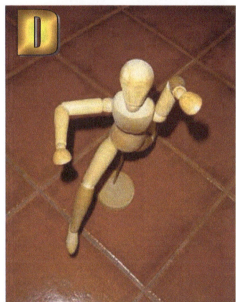

(A, B) TWO SLIGHT VARATIONS OF AN EYE LEVEL

(C) ALMOST FULL WORMS EYE

(D) ALMOST FULL BIRDS EYE

Now, in each of these pictures I want you to notice where the SMILES AND FROWNS are on each one of these manikins.

On the next page is a larger version of this manikin, with the 'SMILES' and "FROWNS" in red.

If you want take your finger and trace over these cuves and get the "FEEL" of the movement of these SMILES and FROWNS.

By doing this you are training your brain to SEE and FEEL these curve on an object. This is called: "MUSCLE MEMORY."

REMEMBER :
BIG TO SMALL

This is important in making sure you can draw the body with the correct perspective depth which is gotten by making sure you have the proper curvilinear degrees of the 'smile' or 'frown.

This goes for as well as clothes won't seem as though the body is wearing them correctly, and they would look pinned on.

So let's take a picture of a person and let's see if you can fill in the blanks.

The camera view is a straight on EYELEVEL, which will be easy to see the smile's and frowns of the clothes, and the joints of this man.

Here is a small quiz. The first answer is given to you…
The top of his head is a…
FROWN
His jaw is a….
His shoulders are…
The shirt neck line is a…
The bottom of his biceps are..
The top of his arm that attaches to his biceps are…
The sleeves are a …
The bottom of the shirt is a ….
The bottom of the shorts are….
The bottom of his calf is…
The bottom of the ankles are a…
The bottom of the shoes are:
HINT on the joint's of the man…look at a manakin.

The next lesson is: "The **PROTRACTOR SPECULATION" THEORY** Using an imaginary or real protractor will provide a shortcut to understand the **DEGEE OF THE CORNER ANGLES** of a box or a rectangle.

ANSWER TO QUESTION: IT IS 'B' BECAUSE THE THE CUP IS TALLER THAN THE OTHER TWO,

CHAPTER 14
"The PROTRACTOR SPECULATION" THEORY

Using an imaginary or real protractor will provide a shortcut to understand the corner angles of a box or a rectangle.

This theory is an off the cuff hypothesis and I thought I'd just throw it in just for an added information.

When you look at a box or table or anything that has corners in a picture I am pretty sure you are NOT wondering, "Gee, I wonder how many degrees, the **'HAPPY Y'**, or **'TIRED T'** arms are spread?" (this theory will be explained in the next chapter, chapter 15.)

That's ok, because your eyes have pretty much told you the APPROXIMATE degrees that these arms are spread.

But, there JUST might come a time when you might be asked to draw a sinister, semi-foggy scene that has one old, war torn wall that has been reduced to a half pile of scattered rubble which at one time used to be a pristine brick wall that kept the enemie out.

Through a lot of research you finally have found a beautiful picture of just what you are looking for. It is perfect and you want to make this picture as accurate as you can and you are one of these people that HAS to be perfect in every aspect of your drawing.

So as you look at this picture, you start realizing that there are angles that need to be correctly depicted, and you know that there are many ways to do this, such as tracing the picture.

But to you, that seems like cheating.

You might graph this piece, but that is time consuming and involves making squares and then painstakingly drawing your piece from one square to another.

Then there is just 'eye-balling' it. But then, for you, as a perfectionist, this isn't going to fly, because you know that your piece won't be what you consider accurate, and there are always the possibilities of the corners being too narrow or too wide throwing your drawing way off.

However, there is another way that usually is not thought of…the protractor.

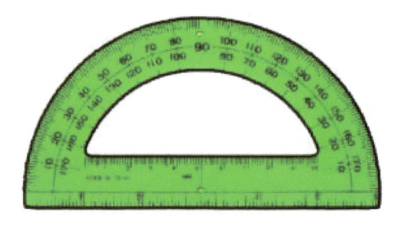

LET'S TAKE A SIMPLE BOX AND USE IT AS AN EXAMPLE.

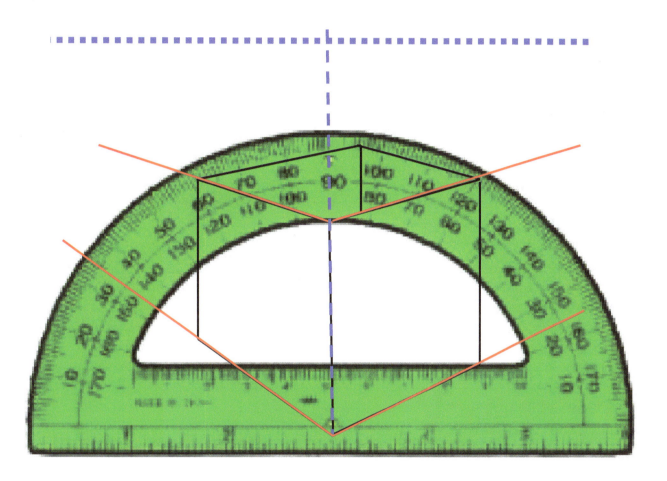

You see that I've lined up the bottom corner of this box on the bottom line next to the 'ruler' part, where the 'hole is and then lined up the front "PILLAR to where it is in line with the 90 degree then taken the "ARMS' OF THE TOP AND BOTTOM of the box and put extensions on them to where these extensions go past the degree numbers

here you see the left bottom line at approx 35 degrees
the top left line 61 degrees
the bottom right line at 155 degrees
and the top right line at 120 degrees

NOW, FOR A PICTURE OF WHAT'S LEFT OF A BRICK WALL….

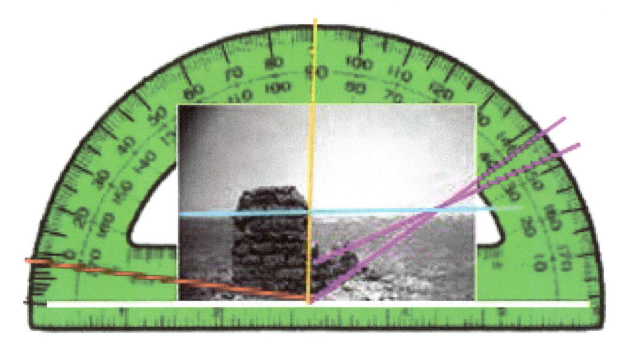

Using your picture reference, you take the protractor and measure the correct angles of the crumbled wall. This gives you a good idea now on the correct angles of the wall spread.' (This picture is taken at a straight on EYE LEVEL.)

This wall is tricky because of the broken layers of the right corner of this wall, so I see that there is the portion of this wall that has not broken, so I will use that CORNER to be the PILLAR to line up on the 90 degree mark which is the exact middle of the protractor. This will be THE PEACH LINE, and what the red and yellow arms degree will be based off of.

The longer orange line is lining up with the 90 degree so that the rest of the angles can use that as a pillar to set their angles.

The white line line is the base of the wall on 'ground zero.

The lower left arm (in red) is apprx 8 degrees*
The lower right arm (in purple is 142 degrees *
The purple TOP arm is 147 degrees.*

The light blue line is the HORIZON LINE it is going through the 20 degree on the left side and 157 on the right side.

 DUE TO THE POOR GRAPHICS ON THE PROTRACTOR THESE STATED DEGREES ARE APPROXIMATED.

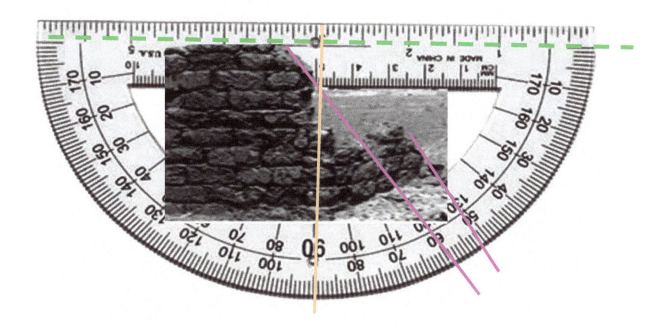

NOW…as you can see, I have the protractor going upright for the "upright" slanted arms… and you can only use the protractor in this upright position for the upright arms in order to get an accurate angle degree for them.

Now will turn the protractor upside down for the to get the downward slant portion of the wall.

As you can see thought, the top of this wall has a " droopy look" so, in order to get an accurate degree for the downward slant of this ruined wall, all one has to do is turn the protractor upside down.

PEACH pillar or edge of the wall up to where the 90 degree is, and the GREEN DOTTED LINE and voila…you will have the correct angles for the DOWNWARD PITCH of the top and back wall."

The TOP OF THE WALL "slant in PURPLE is at 60 degrees (You read the OUTSIDE of the protractor)

The BACK OF THE WALL SLANT…..(GOING AWAY FROM YOU) in PURPLE is 50 degrees.

Here is a simple box to see this downward slant for a better example. So you can see that the right arm is at 10 degrees and the left arm is at 158 degrees.

Now, as I said in the beginning, this theory is only for your 'pleasure' and another tool to put into your tool bag. It probably won't be used a whole lot but, it's there if you need it.

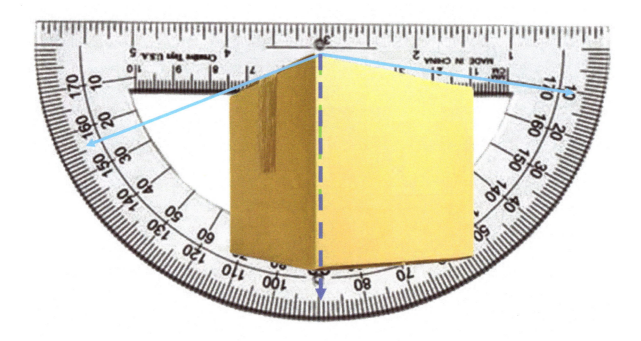

Now onto the next chapter, HAPPY "Y" AND TIRED "T" theory, which is a short cut on finding **WHAT EYE LEVEL** you are looking at, (Birds, Worms, or Straight on Eye Level.), and what degree of wideness the angle is on a box or rectangle that you see from a PICTURE.

CHAPTER 15
THE HAPPY 'Y' & TIRED 'T' THEORY

This is a short cut on finding an angle, and degree of the angle on a box or rectangle that you see from a PICTURE. This helps you tell what depth the camera view is either from a BIRDS EYE ORE WORMS EYE VIEW.

This theory is basically to be used FROM PICTURES

This is a short cut to help those that are having a hard time getting their boxes to stop going up in the air and help them find a correct way of getting them to become 3-DIMENSIONAL on a 2- DIMENSIONAL piece of paper.

This theory also helps to find WHAT view (eye level, birds eye, or worms eye) that the Photographer is using when taking a picture of a box, rectangle or anything that has soft or sharp corners.

In chapter 13 I dealt with curves which showed you how to make sure your curves are correct as you view your object from different camera views.

Now, we will be dealing with recognizing the position of angles on anything square.

I am almost positive that most every artist has gone through the painful experience of drawing boxes that looked like someone sat on them then tipped them up in the air.

This is caused again from trying to fight the 2-DIMENSIONAL paper with a 3-DIMENSIONAL object.

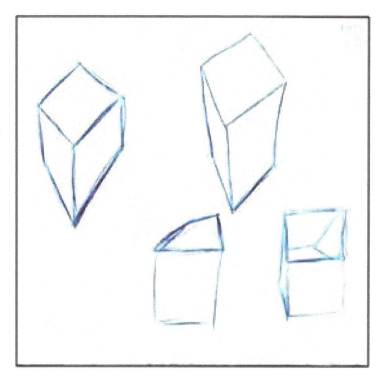

And the paper is winning!

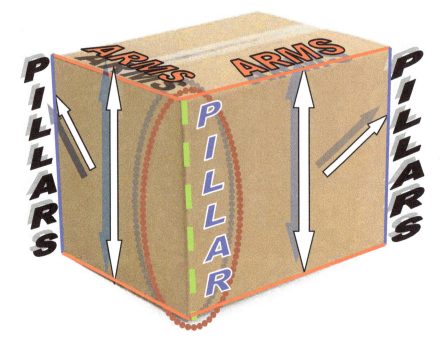

The 'HAPPY Y' will in most cases usually be seen in a BIRDS EYE view.

So, starting with the 'HAPPY here is just a simple ol' box.

The camera view of this box will be a bit more than a ½ view.

Both the red lines look like they are spread in a "HAPPY joyous position and shaped like a Y."

I'm going to again break down the **PHYSICS** of this box and name the <u>VERTICAL AND HORIZONTAL</u> lines and make it easier for you to follow along with this theory.

I am going to ***call*** the VERTICAL lines 'PILLARS.' (Up and down lines)

The front pillar will be colored BLUE & GREEN.

BECAUSE:
The PILLAR that is the CLOSEST to you is the MOST important one.

The other 'pillars' will be colored just BLUE.

This is because the <u>***FRONT PILLAR i***</u>s the where all the 'arms' are going to **HANG** from.

It is the FRONT edge of the square object that you will see FIRST!

I am going to call the HORIZONTAL lines (side to side) "ARMS" and color them RED

DISSECTING THE PARTS OF THE BOX

This is what I will call the "WORKING PILLAR." This is the edge that has **_TWO FUNCTIONS_**

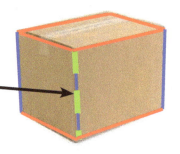

1. It's "IN YOUR FACE" which means that it is the **CLOSEST OBJECT** to you which means it's going to be **ILLUSIONARY BIGGER,** and the rest of the pillars will fade back.

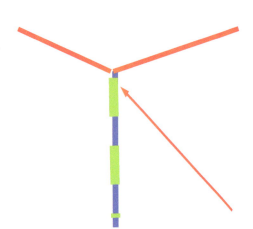

Here you can 'CHEAT' just a LITTLE and draw this pillar a SMIDGEN longer than the rest of the PILLARS, so it gives the illusion of the box going back a bit more than what the picture looks like. (This is drawing WHAT YOU KNOW, NOT WHAT YOU SEE.)

2. The pillar will also be what the top and bottom 'ARMS' will hang off of. Here in this sample you will see why I call this the "HAPPY Y". It's as if they are expressing joy!

THIS IS WHAT YOU WILL SEE WHEN YOU SEE A BOX AT AND ANGLE.

NOT STRAIGHT ON!!! Like this illustration shows.

There will be no 'working pillar's because they've moved to the **SIDE OF THE BOX,** and now have just become **"PILLARS."**

(this will be explained more on the following pages.

Here you can see how all ARMS hang off the corner pillars no matter how the box is turned.

Here is what mistake most beginners do to the ARMS on a ½ bird's eye view. This is what I call… 'STICK 'EM UP' ARMS because the beginner is trying to make the top of the box lay flat on this two dimensional piece of paper but ends up with the 'arms' going straight up in the air.

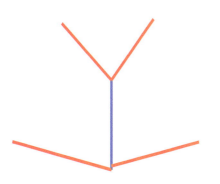

So, the trick to remember is to EXTEND AND LOWER the arms out more and keep the ARMS AND PILLARS parallel to each other and …'SPREAD THE JOY!'

Ok, now there is another problem: *different camera views.* (Is it BIRDS EYE, WORMS EYE OR EYE LEVEL?)

In these three examples *(notice the top plane and how much percentage you're seeing of the surface.)* what is the FIRST THING YOU SEE?

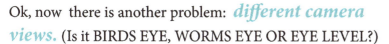

Now what happens when the box is turned straight on?
Uhh, where is the 'WORKING PILLAR?"

This shot is a one point, ¾ birds eye because this box is **almost a straight on** view.
And the camera view is looking at a lot at the TOP of this box.

It is obvious that in this picture that there is no ONE "WORKING PILLAR" because one can see that the
'PILLARS' are equally SPACED and the 'ARMS' are going back.and you do NOT see the side planes of this box.

And the **"HAPPY Y"** is *NOT* there because they are now at a 90 degree angle.

BUT it's the FRONT LINE that needs
to be aware of because it is "IN YOUR FACE" (in pink) because of the illusion of it coming out at you. (especially in this view of looking down upon the box.)

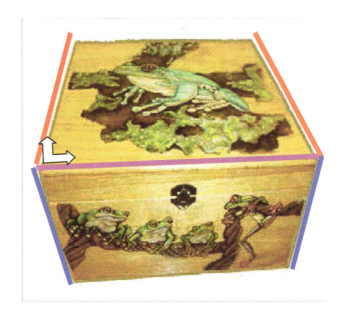

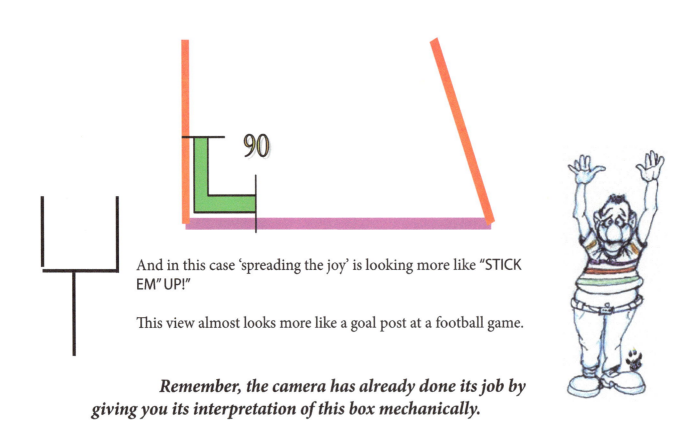

And in this case 'spreading the joy' is looking more like "STICK EM" UP!"

This view almost looks more like a goal post at a football game.

Remember, the camera has already done its job by giving you its interpretation of this box mechanically.

It just captures the image and plunks it on this 2-DIMENSIONAL piece of paper.

It's up to you to interpret what the camera has given you.

This is again a case of what you know…not what you see.

Remember the camera is only a reference tool.

THERE WILL BE SEVERAL WAYS OF LOOKING AT THE "TIRED T"

1. You are looking at a box or angle at a WORMS EYE view as well as a BIRDS EYE view as seen in the illustration below. (The "TIRED T" is in light blue.)

2. All Tired T'S in a Birds Eye eye level will be angling DOWN (the red lines on the top of the top of for the open box is on the boarder line of being a REALLY WIDE "Happy Y" and a beginning of a TIRED T.
3. They are also seen on the back end of the box, cube or anything that is an 'ANGLED' 3-DIMENSIONAL piece.

To help distinguish the 'HAPPY Y' and 'TIRED T' I will make the 'TIRED T' ARMS LIGHT BLUE…FOR SAD.

The PILLARS will always be DARK BLUE

The WORKING PILLAR will be DOTTED GREEN and BLUE

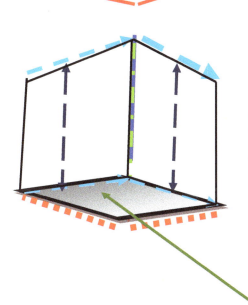

When I first started to draw, I would find myself having a hard time starting a WORMS EYE VIEW that had a 3- DIMENSIONAL look, Meaning that it had a PLANE on the bottom of the box. (in gray)

I am looking just a bit UP at the box And the results of this has forced my brain to start this box with "TIRED T'S"(in light blue)

But that's where it stops because take a look at the bottom of this box.

.It's a wide "HAPPY Y"(IN RED) ! so I have BOTH 'HAPPY Y' and 'TIRED T's"(IN LIGHT BLUE.) BUT…THE MAJORITY OF THIS BOXES ARMS ARE IN A 'TIRED T!" AND A 'HAPPY Y' IS WHEN ONE IS LOOKING DOWN AT THE SQUARE OBJECT IN A BIRDS EYE VIEW (CAMERA VIEW)

I FIND THAT THE RULE OF THUMB FOR A TIRED T SCENARIO IS WHEN ONE IS LOOKING UP AT A SQUARE OBJECT WHICH IS A WORMS EYE VIEW (CAMERA VIEW)

There are **three reasons** why I think this theory of the 'HAPPY Y' and 'TIRED T' is very important

1: because looking at the 'ARM ANGLES of these boxes it's a quick way of being able to differentiate between a bird's eye views vs. a worms eye view.

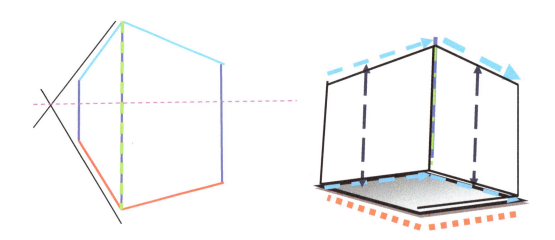

2: Beginners can use this technique to START THEIR BOXES in either the birds eye, or worms eye. And they can control the view of the PLANE on the top or bottom of the box just by spreading the ARMS OF THE BOXES wider or narrower. This helps also in controlling the angle of the box that they are drawing.

3. By controlling the angles of these arms you also control the perspective depth of the box also.

Also you will find that by breaking down the PHYSICS of a box or anything with angles, in this manner, one actually can SEE the differences and be able to draw it with more accuracy.

Can you see the 'TIRED T' in this example

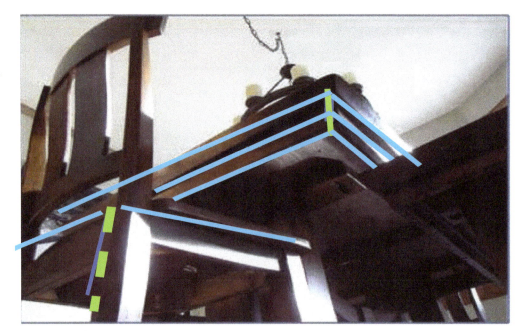

CHAPTER 16
THE COIN THEORY

*This theory will help in drawing the proper perspective on a object that is angled or twisted.
MOST everything you see can usually be divided equally into two parts especially when you are looking at the object straight on.*

The problem starts when you start TURNING the object. Because, as the object turns, the FRONT starts to become "IN YOUR FACE," which means the front is getting bigger, and the back is getting smaller.

Now you will notice that I started out this chapter by saying "MOST." There are ALWAYS exceptions to the rules. I will get into that in a bit. But first I want to further explain this theory.

I named this theory 'THE COIN' THEORY, because using the coin is the quickest and simplest example of finding the center line…

Now let's turn it a bit. Notice how the front half of the quarter is "IN YOUR FACE?"

And the back half is getting smaller.

Ok, that was a simple sample-now for a bit more complicated one.

Let's look at a human that is twisting (this one is interesting because of the muscle structure.) So, where is the center line for all of this mass? It isn't in just one place, it is in several places.

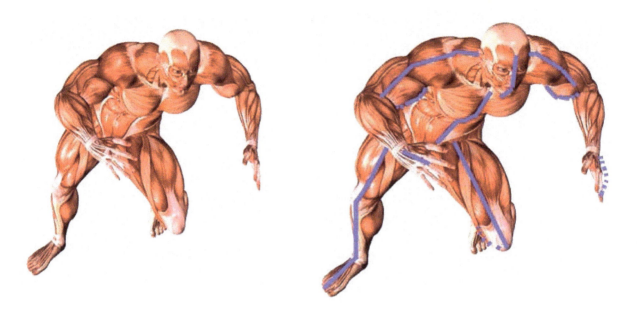

Now you will notice on the lined man, I didn't put a middle line down the lower arms, and that is because the lower arm is one of those tricky areas that one cannot 'middle-ize' because of the ulna and radial bones.

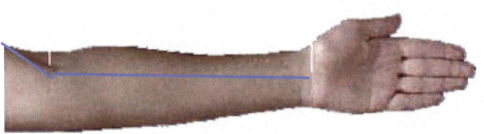

They twist and turn in such a way that they distort the lower arm which makes it almost impossible to get a center line on them.

You will also notice that I 'dotted' the lower leg, and the left hand. That is because in my mind's eye I know and can 'see' the middle line, even if I can't see the lower leg.

If you can 'see' the middle line in your drawings, you then can get the perspective right when a figure is twisted.(This is what I call the GLASS GHOST THEORY which I will get into in chapter 17, the next chapter.)

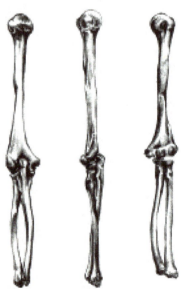

This jumping fox is relatively easy to draw, because he actually looks like a box with four feet.

And in your mind's eye you can 'fly' above him and look down and 'see' his back where you can mentally draw a middle line starting from the tip of the tail to the crown of his head.

In the next chapter the "Glass Ghost theory" you will be further informed on how you can look at the fox as if he were a WIRE FRAME (or glass).

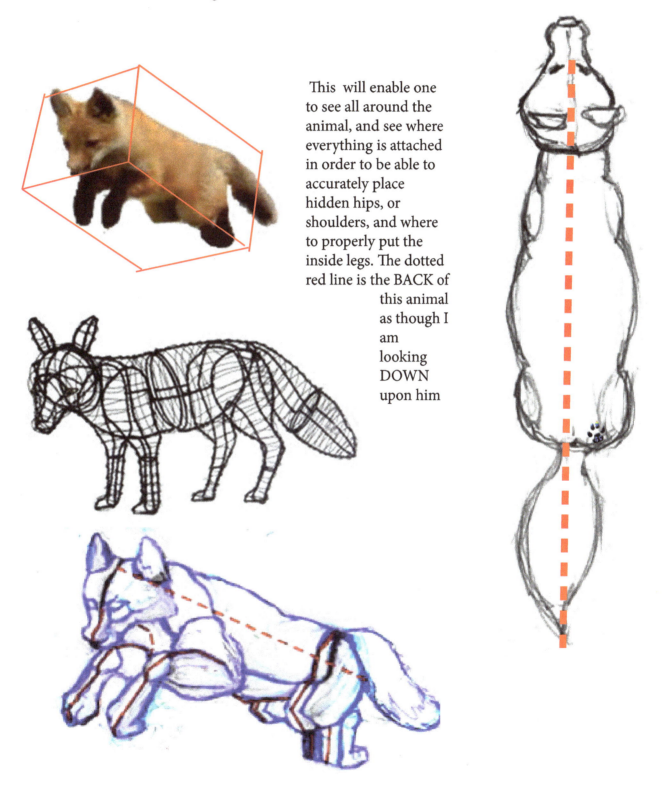

This will enable one to see all around the animal, and see where everything is attached in order to be able to accurately place hidden hips, or shoulders, and where to properly put the inside legs. The dotted red line is the BACK of this animal as though I am looking DOWN upon him

So, there are two things that need to be done to become as accurate as possible:

1. BE ABLE TO LOOK AT THE OBJECT AS A PIECE OF GLASS OR A WIRE FRAME

2. FIND THE MIDDLE LINES OF EVERYTHING THAT CAN BE DIVIDED IN HALF.

There is one more thing to add to this theory, as a review, but it ties into these two very important theories.

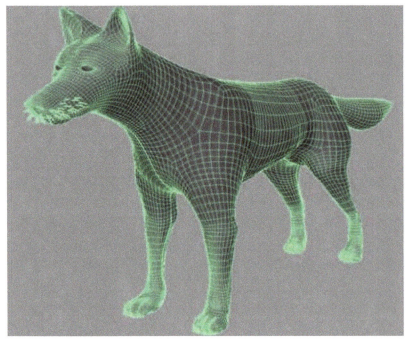

In Book One, "YOU ARE NOW A MICROBE TRAVELING OVER "LUMPY AND BUMPY" you can look at this animated dog, and it is a perfect example of what I am talking about as you use your mental 'hand' to rub all over the contours of this animal.

You will feel the undulations made by the muscles and bones thus creating a mental picture of all the contours.

Notice the line work on this animated dog? See how it curves around shoulders, legs, stomach, neck, and head? This is what I mean by running your mental hand over the object and feeling the 3-DIMENSIONAL curvilinear physics of what you mentally touch.

By doing this, it will further help you in forming a COMPLETE mental picture of what you are drawing and how it 'feels.' in your mind's eye, which will transfer down to your fingers to successfully draw and shade a believable piece of art.

The next lesson is THE GLASS GHOST THEORY which is a lesson on being able to mentally LOOK THROUGH an object to see the other side so you can draw in perspective and accurately, twisted or turned objects.

CHAPTER 17
THE GLASS GHOST THEORY

Being able to see objects all around, and thru this chapter is an important lead in to help you understand the PHYSICAL DEPTH of a form or object.

When you are able to see THROUGH an object as though it were glass, this will: Let you be able to THINK and VISUALIZE in animation (movement) the object you are drawing. And as you can do this, you will be able to move your object up, down, sideways, laying down, standing up, tipped, rearing, and other twisting movements and be able to properly see this object as it would look in these positions in the proper perspective to where all joints, angles, or curves would be anatomically correct, perspectively correct as you view it in the different eye levels (camera views)

This chapter is an important one because it is the polishing now of you becoming an accomplished artist. This chapter is the lead in for the next 3 chapters AND ALSO..a further study of the *previous chapter.

1. "THE COIN THEORY." theory-putting a perspective center line in your drawings (*CHAPTER 16-PREVIOUS CHAPTER.)

2The "SPIDER WEB" theory- making shapes out of the negative spaces in your drawing

3. . "MORPHING DOT to DOT GAME" taking your drawings from a stick figure, to blocks, to cylinders, then connecting everything together.

4. The "BUCKING BRONCO" theory-Movement or ACTION of your piece or of a piece you are looking at.

LEFT SIDE

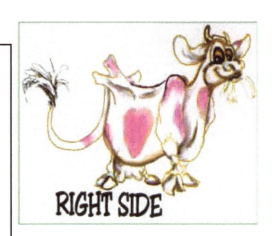
RIGHT SIDE

TOP

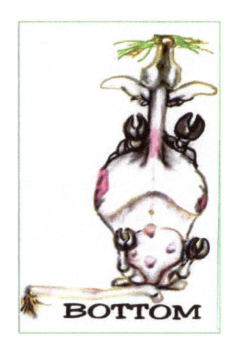
BOTTOM

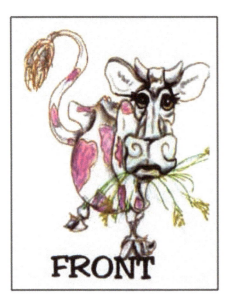
FRONT

BACK

The goal for most artists is to be able to draw without having to look at pictures all the time.

This is what the animator is able to do in the big animation studios such as Disney, Pixar, Warner Brothers, Hanna-Barbera and DreamWorks.

This is what you must be able to do if you are also to illustrate comic books, or graphic novels, become a cartoonist, or political cartoonist.

As an accomplished artist, you should be able to take most any subject and be able to see it at all angles. When this happens you will be free to draw anything that your mind thinks up.

You still will need references, for the brain does not have all the answers!

The best way to REALLY understand the subject matter, especially if it an animal, or human is to study the anatomy thoroughly.

Know what the muscles do, and the differences of muscle groups between animal and human. This will help you

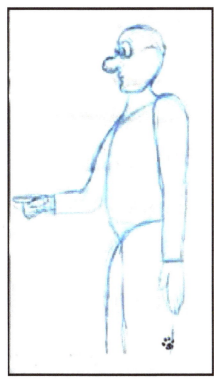

Ok, now, I am going to ask you a question here, I am sure that most of you beginning artists have at one time or the other attempted to draw a human that is standing either at a full side view, or at a ¾ side view.

Let's say you want this arm raised, and the hand is pointing at something. So, you draw it, and when you finish you look at it and realize that the shoulder is way too low.

And you are drawing right along just knocking out this figure quite nicely, until it comes time to draw the other arm and hand.

So you hunch the back a bit to try and make the shoulder and the back meet equally, nope.
Now your drawing is taking on the beginning look of the "Ghoul from Zanzibar."
So you now raise the shoulder line to meet the neck line…

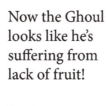

Now the Ghoul looks like he's suffering from lack of fruit!

So, in desperation you now take the front shoulder, shorten it to where the shoulder line meets the neck to try and match the other shoulder.

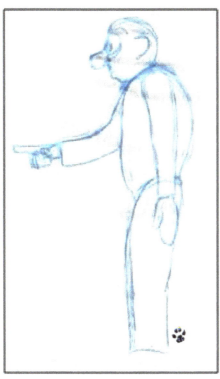

Now the Ghoul looks like he's melting from the heat and lack of fruit..so, you give up, and in disgust, walk away

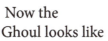

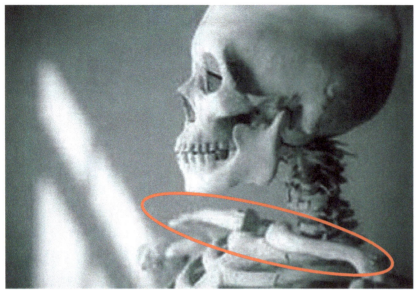

Don't feel bad, this is exactly what happened to me, and it took me ages to figure out just what was going on. Of course I did this without really knowing the human anatomy. So, I was winging it.

Making mistake after mistake until, I realized that one: I needed to take the bull by the horns and study the human anatomy.

And two, I best be like superman and be able to look through muscle and bone to see what was on the other side of the body, and see where everything is in relativity to the side I can see.

But of course, this wasn't going to happen until I looked at an anatomy book and studied the human body.

Ok, so let's take another look at the *"Ghoul from Zanzibar,"* and try and morph him back into a decent looking fellow…

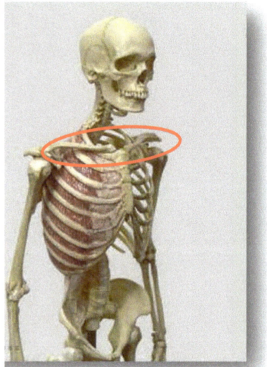

The trick is to take a look at the shoulder that is " IN YOUR FACE" and then look through the neck as if it were glass, and follow through your imagination, the collar bone to the other side of the body…

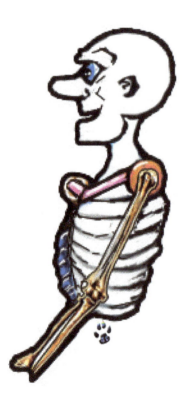

Now, in order to see THROUGH the skeleton, to the other side, and see the WHOLE body you need to take a, little trip around the whole body to see every angle…but this will be in your mind's eye. And for this you will need, two things…

1. A good pictorial reference anatomy book that shows you every angle
.2. PRACTICE, and studying the anatomy of the human or animal , and memorizing where the joints are in comparison to other parts of the body.

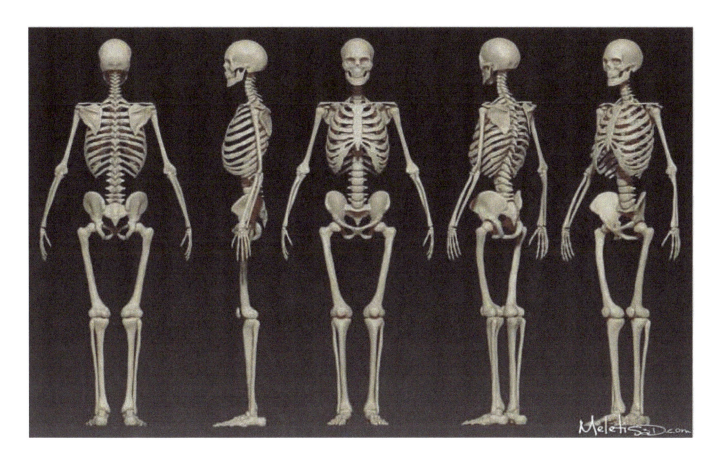

Ok, now that you have a pretty good idea of what I'm talking about here, let's go on to the next theory.

the "SPIDER WEB THEORY." The Study of looking at the 'negative' shapes within the positive shapes to achieve accuracy when copying a picture.

Remember: PRACTICE, PRACTICE, PRACTICE!!!!! THIS ISN'T GOING TO COME TO YOU OVER NIGHT!

CHAPTER 18
The SPIDER WEB" theory

The Study of looking at the 'negative' shapes within the positive shapes to achieve accuracy when coping a picture.

Have you ever copied a picture and you **REALLY, REALLY, REALLY** want it to look EXACTLY like what you are copying without tracing the picture?

Well, most of the time you are going to get really, really close, but there will always be some differences just because you are you, and your style of drawing is going to dictate how your picture will turn out…

REMEMBER: EVERYONE HAS A DIFFERENT STYLE NO MATTER HOW THEY COPY OR TRY AND EMULATE THEIR FAVORITE ARTIST. YOUR PICTURE USUALLY WILL NOT BE THE EXACT, BANG ON, PERFECT REPLICA OF WHAT YOU SEE.

You will always be off just that little bit that changes the image of what you see, because of your style and interpretation…so realize this and just do the best you can.

Meanwhile though, as you are copying your picture you become aware of little things that are off such as the subtle curve in the shoulder, or the position of the arm is not just right, or the legs might be spread out too wide, and no matter how you try and work it, the drawing just looks "OFF."

Ok, there is a trick that can help you get that 'just-right' angle, or curve.

In a drawing, you are going to have what is called, "Positive, and Negative' spaces.

The positive space is what you are drawing.

The Negative spaces are the blank spaces that you didn't draw, and the space that has been created by the positive art work.

Now, let's take this picture, and I will show you two examples on how to look at these negative shapes.

Now, if you draw the cat and the objects it is holding the best way you know how, then once it's drawn, take a look at your negative spaces, and see if they match your negative SHAPES.

IE…look at the bottom right foot, the one that is sticking out at you.(where the dotted green oval is,).then look at the pink dotted line see how it has formed a TRIANGLE NEGATIVE SHAPE between the top of the foot to the slight bulge of the haunch.

On this sample by coloring all the negative shapes green, the negative shapes are very obvious.

Now, on to the " **BUTTERFLY MORPHING THEORY**", taking a stick drawing and adding FLAT, 2-D squares, rectangles, circles and triangles onto it, then "morphing' these 2-D shapes into 3-D shapes which now become blocks, pyramids, spheres, and cylinders.

Then 'playing' dot to dot' and connecting all of these with the right curvatures in order to complete your figures, or objects.

CHAPTER 19
"THE BUTTERFLY MORPHING" THEORY

Taking a stick drawing adding 2-d squares, rectangles, circles and triangles onto it, then "morphing' these 2-d shapes into 3-d blocks, pyramids, spheres, & cylinders. Then 'playing' dot to dot' and connecting all of these with th right curvatures in order to complete your figures, or object

There are lots of steps that many beginning artists don't want to follow because it's human nature to just jump right in and draw the full figure .
\
Art is looking at a lot of things, but one has to start out with the BASICS…
The general rule is that all OBJECTS ARE MADE UP OF SHAPES.

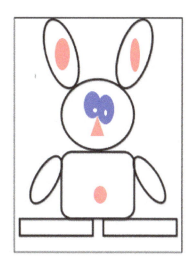

It is your job as an artist to see these shapes and then put them together.

The reason why I call this theory

is because like a butterfly, this insect starts out as an egg, then a caterpillar, then it spins a cocoon, where it soon emerges into a fully blown, beautiful butterfly.

Drawing objects either from a picture, or a real object has the same steps that you need to follow in order to get you picture to come out as a beautiful, perspectivly correct and believable drawn object.

By looking at an object as shapes first, this helps to prevent looking at the object as a finished object which a lot of times for a beginner can be a bit overpowering and daunting.

Let's take a look at this picture of this cougar and you will see how taking simple shapes I will build a manikin animal using simple shapes.

So, as you can see shapes can pretty well map out your object to where now all that's left is to 'connect the dots,' round out everything, and put in the details.

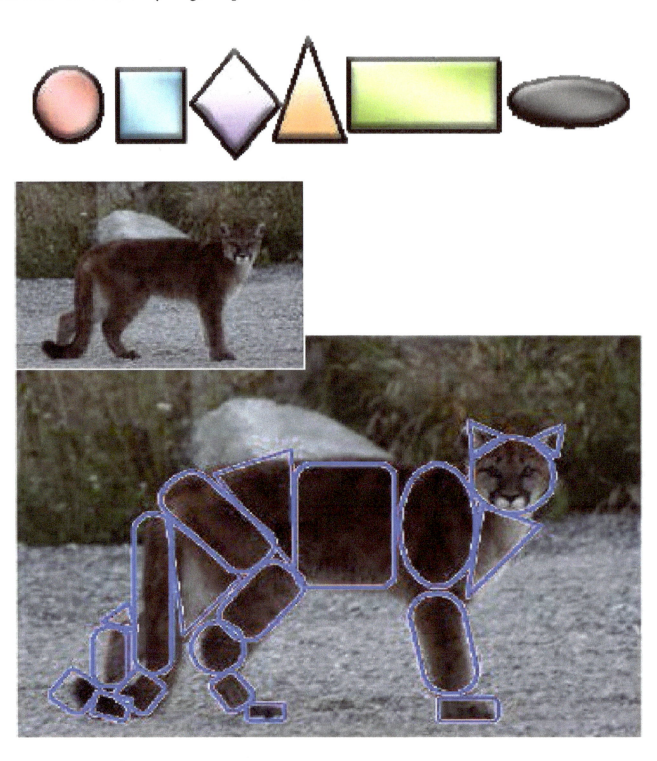

Now on the next page is five (5) steps to get the proper action and perspective to your picture. These steps, if used, will accurately make your piece come out as close as possible to the picture or realistic object you are drawing.

Just remember one thing, every artist has their own different 'fingerprint and style, so if several people were to be drawing the same picture, they all will come out a bit differently even when following these steps. That is what makes art so wonderful, and this doesn't mean that you are not a good artist! So get that out of your head right now!

Step one: draw the action line,

Step two: draw the stick figure, (which is the 'wire frame' of your piece.)

Step three: 2-d block out shapes such as circles, rectangles, boxes, triangles, to fit onto the stick figure. (This is the birth of the manikin.)

Step four: then 3-D these simple shapes into blocks, spheres, rectangles, cones, and cylinders, (making sure now that the proportions of the body are correct, you can use a reference book, or go online to study this) now you have made a good solid manikin which to go onto step five to finish your body.

Step five: connect all of these shapes now with the correct joint angles, and finish off the picture.

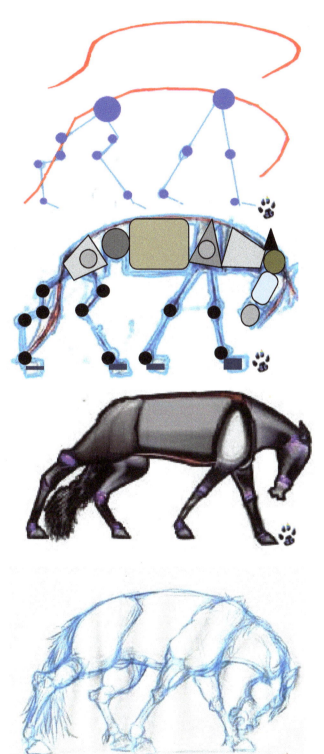

There is one more thing, which is important for you to pay attention to with step five, and this has to do with CAMERA VIEW. (birds eye, worms eye, or straight on eye level.)

You need to watch the angles of the curves on the top and bottom of the cylinders because this has a lot to do with HOW the curves in the joints are going to wrap around the 'ball' or joints. Which will get your drawing perspectivly right. R*EMEMBER CHAPTER THIRTEEN, THE SMILE AND FROWN THEORY*
The picture below is a shot of a manikin at EYE LEVEL. (You are looking straight at it) I have circled the angles of the cylinders around the joint "balls" see how they curve!

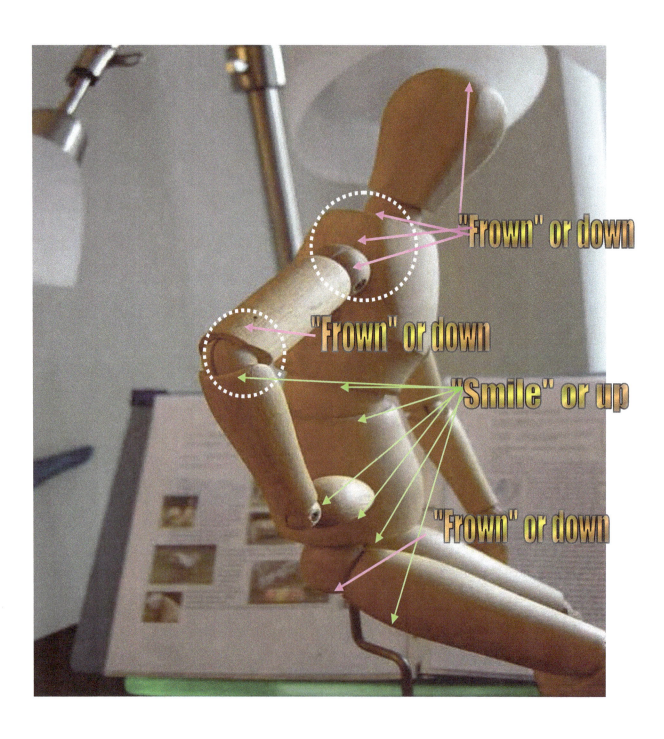

There is one more area I want you to look at: See the arrow at the bottom of the head?

This I call the **'GRAY AREA'** on the top right and left leg joint.)

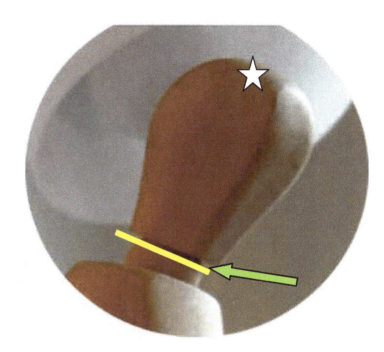

Notice how the 'curve' could be a question of whether it is either smile or frown? (this is because you are looking straight at this line.) well, now you need to draw **NOT WHAT YOU SEE BUT WHAT YOU KNOW!!!**

think back to CHAPTER ELEVEN- "YOU ARE NOW A MICROBE." THEORY, .and you know that this head is NOT FLAT but ROUND.

So you are now going to take a trip and travel AROUND the head.

Look at where the 'APEX' of the curve (where the star is on the head) is or exact middle of the curve, or the highest point which means that this is the HIGHEST point in the curve and it is coming OUT AT YOU!!! In your face!

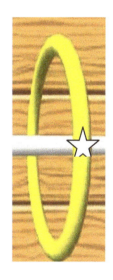

Think of traveling up a hill and reaching the top (APEX) of the hill, then going down the hill, reaching the APEX or point of the bottom of the hill before it starts going BACK UP the hill. But there is an APEX in the middle of that hill which is the exact point where it starts to change directions.

Now you have a choice. You are looking at this point of the head at a straight on shot, the straight or 'EYE LEVEL.' BUT, this is where you can **"CHEAT"** a bit and curve this bottom line at the base of the head into a SMALL SMILE, meaning that you will curve the line UP JUST A BIT. What this will do is give you a bit more animation or 3-dimensional to the head making it look like it is pooching out just a bit, which will be quite helpful when it gets shaded.

This process of thinking is extremely important because as you shade this piece that you become aware of the **PHYSICS OF LUMPY AND BUMPY"**

(CHAPTER 10.) and be able to shade the piece as a ROUND object giving it the feeling of 3-dimension instead of shading it straight across which will give it a flat look.

So, in this chapter I think you are beginning to see how all the other chapters are starting to fit into making your piece look real, and how to THINK in 3-d.

The next chapter is a very important one, for it is the study
of Movement. I call this chapter,
"THE BUCKING BRONCO" THEORY,
which will be, The study of seeing and drawing
dynamic **"LINE OF ACTION"**

CHAPTER 20
"THE BUCKING BRONCO" THEORY

The Study of seeing and drawing dynamic "Line of action" movement in your drawings.

I have called this theory the " Bucking Bronco" theory, because bucking broncos and the passenger aboard usually is in a high degree of twisting and turning and what better example to show
MOVEMENT?

When a student starts drawing more than likely they are not paying attention to the dynamics of the piece that they are drawing. And when they finish the picture, it shows.

It is usually cardboard stiff, and lacks 'character,' excitement, and MOVEMENT.

In the art world a quickie definition of MOVEMENT is what is known as "LINE OF ACTION."as was discussed

"Line of action is usually a curved line that runs from one end of an action figure to the other and a lot of time's there is more than one "Line of Action."

So, just for kicks let's draw two versions of someone eating an ice cream cone. Which line shows more 'enthusiasm?' more eye candy? And is -

NOT BORING?

If you chose the dude that is enthusiastically slurping down his dripping, three-decker ice cream cone, you now have earned yourself a chocolate, double fudge dipped caramel, three scoop, ice cream cone.

 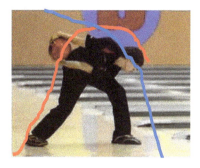 

The "line of action" should be used to start a picture which will help you get the movement going in the right direction. Then you can start drawing around this line of action.

Also there might come a time too, that you are wanting to draw a nifty action figure, but you have absolutely NO idea how to start, or how the figure should be posed, so you can also take your pencil and scribble some squiggles onto your paper, (not too squiggly, but loose "loopty-loop" lines) this should help you "SEE" a figure doing SOMETHING!

And if you have a picture you want to draw from then DRAW the action lines on the picture!

The picture is not sacred! (Unless it's a picture of your great grandfather Frank back in the good ol' days, and if that is the case get a copy of it, then draw on that copy to your heart's content.

It is important to make sure this character isn't boring! So, let's say I want to do a basketball player doing a major slam dunk.

STEP ONE: I've drawn a pretty ELONGATED backward 'C'

STEP TWO, I can envision where the arms and legs are going to go, and the small bump at the top of this 'C' gives me the idea of how I have to exaggerate the chest.

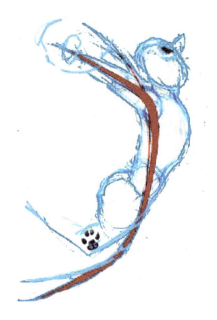

STEP THREE: Now can start working the body, as a sketchy 'blueprint' of what the finished piece will look like.

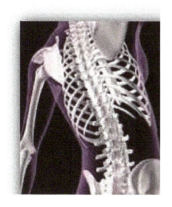 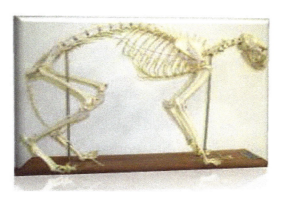 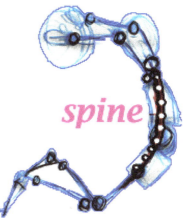

Remember in both the animal and human anatomy the 'pillar' of your drawing is the SPINE.

Then you can take these shapes and envision where the spine of the animal or human is and then work the action figure from that **IN STICK FORM FIRST** then build the figure from there.

This method is used not only for cartoonists and animators, but all artists that are drawing action figures and are using pictures as a guide.

In these pictures can you find the action lines? There can be more than one

The next chapter will be **"WHY ARE YOU LOOKING AT YOUR THUMB?"** theory which is,

understanding how to look at real objects and then by using a straight object such as a pencil or stick, (or your thumb in an emergency) to be able to draw these objects accurately.

CHAPTER 21
"WHY ARE YOU LOOKING AT YOUR THUMB" THEORY

Understanding how to look at real objects and then by using a straight object such as a pencil or stick, (or your thumb in an emergency) you will be able to draw these objects accurately.

I know that you have seen many cartoon gags on a person holding out his arm and seeming to take aim with their thumb at the object in front of them, Well, this isn't too far from the truth, for the thumb IS a form of measurement.

Have you been in an art class with a still life in front of you with a plethora of various different objects, shapes and sizes and become overwhelmed on where to begin? And have asked your teacher,
"HOW DO I START THIS? "

And the answer is ' *JUST START ANYWHERE! AND JUST DRAW WHAT YOU SEE!*"

Well I have had that experience and the results of my efforts weren't pretty… because left to my own devices, I found that all the objects ran off the paper, the perspective wasn't right, the object sizes did not jive with the other objects, and it looked FLAT!

I had to learn the hard way.

Basically the first problem was that I didn't start the piece on the paper in the right position which would have given me the correct room I needed to fit in all of these items.

Basically the first problem was that I didn't start the piece on the paper in the right position which would have given me the correct room I needed to fit in all of these items.

As a greenhorn, I started somewhere on the top of the page thinking I was going to need the bottom to fit in all the items that were in the still life. When I did this, the still-life was crammed up at the top of the page leaving a huge margin on the bottom of the page.

I knew about the 'thumb' thing, but I didn't understand it, and I believe it was because my art teacher threw '50 million objects' at me to draw instead of just ONE item and telling us to "just draw what you see!" "

Ok, so my question was, 'OK, I SEE a pile of different objects but where do I start?"

I had to learn this the hard way by watching my students become frustrated and realizing that you cannot throw nine million items at them and expect them to understand how to do successful render all of them on the paper properly.

I had to learn that by teaching my students to draw just ONE ITEM at a time was the key to success.

And usually starting them out with a simple bottle like the one on the right.

But…This bottle is not as easy as it looks because it's hard to get the top curves equal.

Once the student understands the physics of the simple bottle I like them to do one that is square with definite angles that defines the body of the bottle .
These will be the clues or the landmarks that will use to measure properly and accurately what they are drawing.

 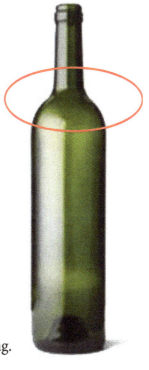

Now, to explain how this phenomena works using your thumb or better yet...a straight object such as a pencil, or a small stick or dowel, is going to be difficult but, here it goes...

There are three methods that artists can use when drawing from real life, and photo shots.

1. *DRAWING BY EYE,* is definitely fine when you are doing sketch work, but I do not recommend it if doing a finished piece especially if trying to get accuracy.

2. *SIGHTING WITH TOOL* - Using a tool for measurement, this will give your picture the beginning accuracy

3. *GRAPHING* - using a plastic piece with 1 inch or ½ squares etched into it, then drawing 2 inch squares on your canvas or paper to blow up your work, and then using what's inside the squares as a guide to accurately draw a replica on your canvas. This method is used mostly if you want to copy a photograph accurately.

A. Set the bottle on a stool, or table,
B. Slide your chair back about 5 or 6 feet with pad in lap.
C. draw on your pad a straight line which will indicate the middle of the bottle.
D. Take your stick and hold it in your fist with your thumb on the side of the stick.
E. Raise your arm with stick in hand straight out in front of you.
F. Close one eye and .sight with stick onto the bottle.
then go to your paper and hold that measurement, place your thumb on the stick where you have just sighted for the top of the bottle, then go to your paper and 'eyeball approx. 2 to 4 inches down from the top of the paper and put a mark IN THE MIDDLE OF THE PAPER. (make a mark on it. This will indicate the TOP of the bottle.
G. then from that mark you will draw a long straigh line, this will indicate the middle of the bottle and will be the object to where you are going to be making your marks for measuring.
H. Then take your stick once again sight on top of the bottle then SLIDE YOUR THUMB down the stick to where the BOTTOM of the bottle hold that mark.
I. Go back to your paper and place the top of the stick on the top of the line you just drew, and then place the stick flat on the paper keeping your thumb on the stick whre you measured for the bottom of the bottle..
MAKE A MARK. You now have the measuremts for the start of the bottle of which you are going to build on.

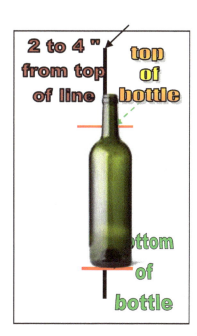

You have just measured the FULL height of the bottle. This is done in ONE STEP!
J. Now measure from the top of the bottle to the bottom of the neck just before the curve starts to go in make

A MARK.(PART ONE)

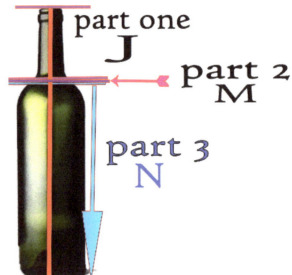

M. Then measure from the bottom
of the neck to the spot
where the curve starts to straighten out
on the base of the bottle.
Make a mark.(PART TWO)

N. Measure then from this
line to the bottom of the
bottle which will give you
the distance you will need
for the body of the bottle.
PART THREE

K. Now, turn the pencil sideways and measure the width
of the body of the bottle and the neck of the bottle
you will have to do this in two parts

O. Now you can measure by pencil, or EYE the two top ridges of the bottle.(where the cap goes) You are now ready to draw the bottle.

P. Using these measurements, you will finish the bottle off by just following your markings. And when the LINE drawing of the bottle is done, you can finish it off by using your eye to complete any markings, or inside shapes that are in the bottle. Then shade it if you want.

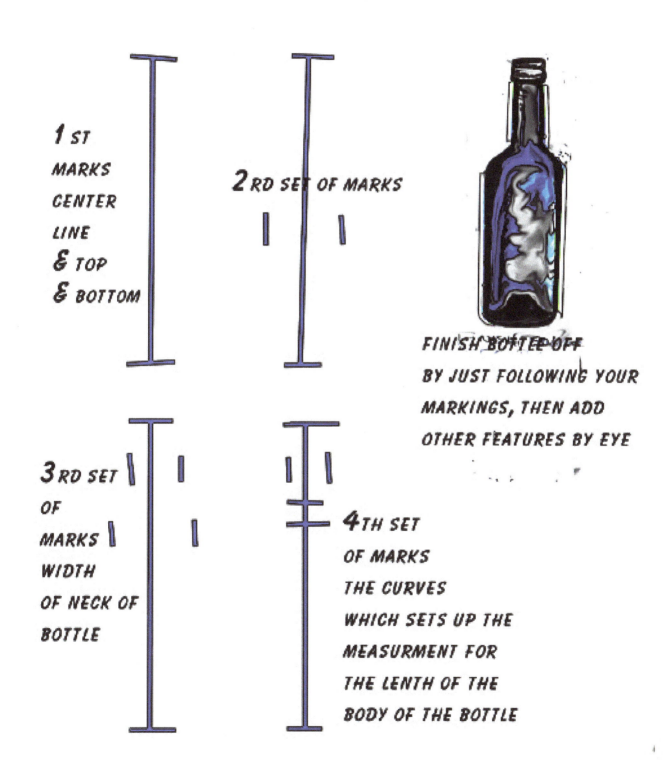

CHAPTER 22
IN CONCLUSION AND SUMMARY

Art, once you know it and understand the concepts of it will seem pretty easy.

But like all things you tackle it will take patience and time.

There is a lot to know in this book, so, what I would like to do is summarize the steps that you had to go through in order to start becoming the Michelangelo I know you can be.

There were two segments of the book:

WHICH THE FIRST RULE, I CALLED

WHICH CONSIST OF:

DIMENSION

*1 dimension
2 dimension
3 dimension

VANISHING POINTS

1 point
2 point
3 point

CAMERA VIEW (AKA: EYE LEVEL)

Eye level
Bird's eye
Worms eye

"HORIZON LINE (AKA: EYE LEVEL) AND HOME BASE" FOR VANISHING POINT'S

Eye level
Bird's eye
Worms eye

These rules were the foundation of your "ART HOUSE" for without the understanding of these rules, you will end up struggling needlessly floundering about trying to get your picture to look real or three dimensional on a two dimensional piece of paper.

Then onto:

The MAGICAL Illusion of Perspective

which consists of that dreaded word:

PHYSICS

...Which is not the hard core mathematical physics that rocket scientists use to get the space shuttle up. But, the **PHYSICS of ART**, which is the ==**SOLID MASS**== that everything you see is made of.

And, through the study of how physics works one becomes aware of how the forces of nature causes different gradations of light and dark, tints and tones, smooth and rough, and up's and downs which makes your work come alive and 3-dimensional.

BUT...In the world of art we look at an object in its *entirety*, because it is necessary to stave off the mind boggling ...

In the beginning, this is a constant struggle to get your favorite picture to look real on a flat piece of paper.

The word you need to know is called:

ART IS THE MAGIC OF ILLUSION! BUT LIKE A MAGICIAN, THE ARTIST MUST KNOW how to create a three dimensional (h, w, d) ILLUSION on a PIECE OF FLAT 2-DIMENSIONAL (HEIGHT AND WIDTH) PAPER

dimension consists of:

IS THERE A ONE DIMENSION?

1 DIMENSION:

If dimension is HEIGHT, WIDTH, DEPTH, then what is **one dimension**?
Is it a dot, line, or a slit?
No, *for they all have some sort of height and width, so there is* **NOT** *an* **ARTISTIC** *1 dimension.*

TWO DIMENSION

2 dimension is HEIGHT, AND WIDTH.
The most common 2 dimensional <u>ART</u> *object is a piece of paper, or a canvas, that you draw on.*

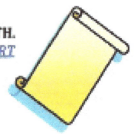

THREE DIMENSION

3-DIMENSION IS: HEIGHT+WIDTH+DEPTH.
Three dimension gives the illusion of realism to the object that you are drawing on your piece of paper. The three dimension illustion is usually accomplished by turning your piece at a ¾ view, and placing it where you can **see a side, a top, or bottom depending how and where you are looking**.

Dimention does not stand by itself, it needs help...*so what are the 'helpers' that dimention needs to achieve a three-dimentional look?*

THERE ARE 5 MAJOR HELPERS
ONE

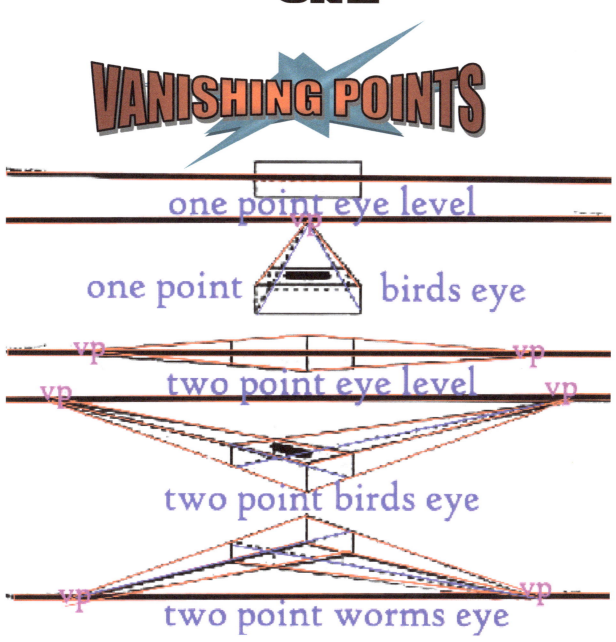

VANISHING POINTS gives this **DIMENSION** the illusion of giving the image height, width, depth which in turn gives your picture **REALITY**...

This is a hard lesson to understand because you have to wade through several steps of vanishing points...

2.
VANISHING POINTS HAVE 3 DIFFERENT "POINTS"
ONE POINT
TWO POINT

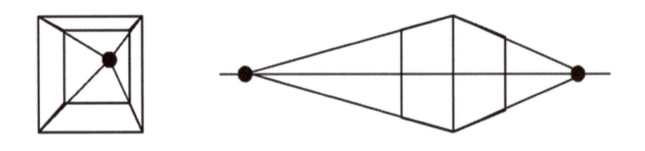

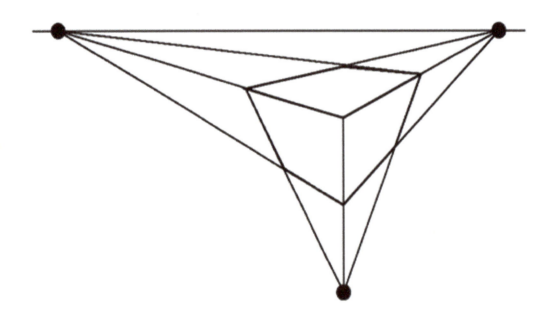

THREE POINT

3.

But there is a bit more to this than just these three points and this is where it gets confusing: because these three vanishing points are determined on **WHERE** you are looking… I call this step:

CAMERA VIEW WHICH IS CALLED IN ARTISTIC LINGO…. "EYE LEVEL"

4. Now, this **CAMERA VIEW** has another name…
"EYE LEVEL." which are listed below…. This is the step that will establish the three dimensional DEPTH, height and width of your drawings.

THIS IS THE PART THAT USUALLY WILL FLUMMOX MOST ARTISTS.

Because there are so many views that can be seen depending on where you are looking and each one of these views has a name.

(I have found that the most confusing and hardest part of learning something usually involves the most complicated rules… and this is one of them! So don't get discouraged…)

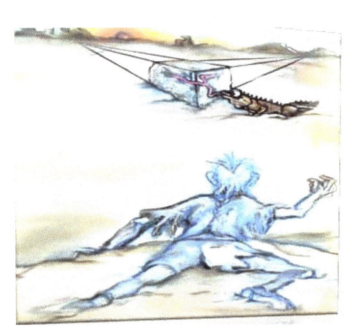

EYE LEVEL (NO VANISHING POINTS…looking straight at the object.)
ONE POINT BIRDS EYE-
(¼, ½, ¾, AND FULL)
ONE POINT WORMS EYE
(¼, ½, ¾, AND FULL)
TWO POINT BIRDS EYE…
(¼, ½, ¾, AND FULL)
TWO POINT WORMS EYE
(¼, ½, ¾, AND FULL)
THREE POINT, TWO POINT, BIRDS- EYE
(¼, ½, ¾, AND FULL)
THREE POINT, TWO POINT WORMS EYE
(¼, ½, ¾. AND FULL)…

Now all these depth lines has to go somewhere, and in most cases they will cross at one point, and where they cross is what I will call:

"HOME BASE"

BUT….

THE REAL ARTISTIC TERM OF 'HOME BASE IS……

"HORIZON LINE."

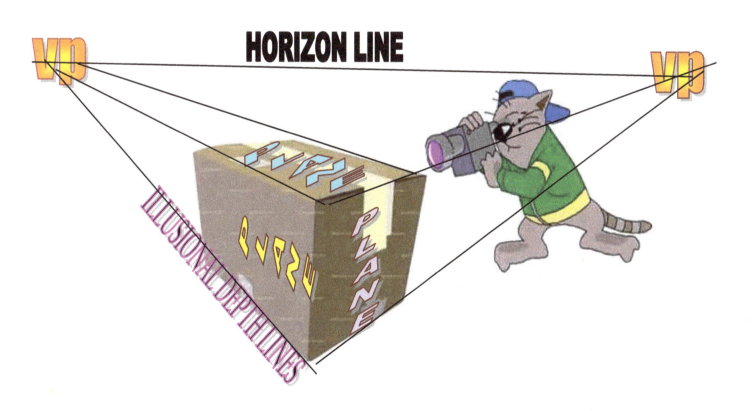

SO TO SUM THE FIRST BOOK ALL UP...

In other words, **DIMENSION** cannot be achieved unless you have **VANISHING POINTS**, and **VANISHING POINTS** establishes the **HORIZON LINE**.

But All of the above rules cannot be achieved unless you have <u>*an understanding on where the photographer is focusing the camera on the main subject if one is going to use a PICTURE to draw from)*</u>)

<u>which I call: CAMERA VIEW</u>

<u>and the accepted artistic term is:</u>

<u>EYELEVEL</u> <u>*if you are using your eyeballs to establish your view in REAL scenery*</u>

The second part of this book is taking these RULES, and applying them to :
As you have read through this book I think that you have found that everything so far is tying everything together one step at a time.

Maybe you can remember all these **RULES** in a song which sort of goes like the song of:

"DEM BONES! -DEM BONES"

"the foot bone is connected to the leg bone, and the leg bone is connected to the thigh bone, the thigh bone is connected to the hip bone" etc…

VERSE ONE,   BOOK ONE

UNDERSTANDING ART is connected to 'RULES AND THEORIES.

Rules and theories are connected to PHYSICS.

Physics is CONNECTED TO the 3-D DRAWING ON a FLAT 2-D PAPER…

3-D DRAWING ON a FLAT 2-d PAPER IS CONNECTED TO DIMENSION

DIMENSION IS CONNECTED TO the CAMERA VIEW of an object…

The CAMERA VIEW of an object is connected to the objects DEPTH LINES

Depth lines establishes VANISHING POINTS…

VANISHING POINTS establish the HORIZON LINE…

END OF THE 'RULES

SECOND PART OF THIS BOOK IS :
THEORIES

VERSE TWO BOOK TWO

THE PHYSICS OF LUMPY AND BUMPY 'CONNECTS to **BECOMING A MICROBE,**

BECOMING A MICROBE CONNECTS TO THE **COFFEE CUP THEORY** "

THE COFFEE CUP THEORY IS CONNECTED TO THE THE **"SMILE & FROWN**

"THE "*THE SMILE AND FROWN*" IS CONNECTED TO THE… **"PROTRACTOR SPECULATION…"**

THE "*PROTRACTOR SPECULATION* IS CONNECTED TO THE **"HAPPY "Y" & TIRED "T…**

THE 'HAPPY Y" AND TIRED T' IS CONNECTED TO THE **COIN THEORY…**

THE "COIN THEORY IS CONNECTED TO THE "**GLASS GHOST "THEORY…**

THE "*GLASS GHOST*" THEORY IS CONNECTED TO THE **" SPIDER-WEB" THEORY…**

"*SPIDER- WEB* " THEORY IS CONNECTED TO THE **"BUTTERFLY MORPHING THEORY"…**

THE "*BUTTERFLY MORPHING*" THEORY IS CONNECTED TO THE **"BUCKING BRONCO THEORY.**

THE BUCKING BRONCO THEORY" IS CONNECTED TO THE "**WHY ARE YOU LOOKING AT YOUR THUMB" THEORY**

"*WHY ARE YOU LOOKING AT YOUR THUMB*" THEORY IS the

END OF SONG …AND….
END OF BOOK TWO
&
END OF BOOK

Here is some sage advice from an article that pertains to Artists, but I am going to take the liberty of taking out Artists" to Artists, for this advice is just the same.
The article is called:

TWO ESSENTIAL WORDS FOR ARTISTS

That is all excellent, but today, I'm giving you the only two words that matter: beyond all advice, beyond all classes, beyond all books and blogs,

DON'T QUIT.

Don't Quit (Even When Nobody Else "Gets" It)

You can only truly fail if you quit, so keep drawing!
—Bryan Hutchinson

It's easy to say "don't quit." It's harder to follow through in real life.
- When your trusted friend sees your work and tells you it's not good, don't quit.
- When you get the fifth (or fiftieth or five-hundredth) rejection from an art gallery don't quit.
- When your art doesn't even place in that contest, don't quit.

Your drawing idea is like a seed—and sometimes, you're the only one who can imagine the future tree. This is normal. This is also one of the most painful phases of creation. During the period of time when no one else can understand what you're doing, it's absolutely essential not to give up. Your art-seed needs time to grow.

DON'T QUIT (EVEN WHEN IT'S HARDER THAN YOU THOUGHT)

Keep moving forward.
—Walt Disney
- When finishing that drawing takes longer than you hoped, don't quit.
- When you realize you have more to learn than you ever dreamed, don't quit.
- When comic book or graphic artist literary agents or editors tell you your idea isn't ready for publication, don't quit.

ART TAKES TIME!!!!!

LEARNING TO DO ART WELL TAKES PERSISTENCE.

How hard can it be to do art ? As it turns out, very hard—but that doesn't mean it isn't worth the struggle. You'll run into roadblocks, look back on older drawings with some embarrassment (hopefully a good sense of humor), and struggle to incorporate new techniques. This is normal. There's a learning curve for anything worth doing, and your art definitely falls into that category.

Don't Quit (Even When It Seems Impossible)

Don't quit. It's very easy to quit during the first 10 years. Nobody cares whether you do art or not, and it's very hard to do art when nobody cares one way or the other. You can't get fired if you don't do art, and most of the time you don't get rewarded if you do. But don't quit.
Andre Dubus

- **When you feel like you're drawing in a vacuum and no one cares, don't quit.**
- **When you feel like your career to do art will never be what you wanted, don't quit.**
- **When you feel like it's hopeless, a pit with no bottom, a road with no end,**

DON'T QUIT.

You're going to make mistakes. You're going to get lost in the drawing labyrinth and struggle to find your way out (and probably have to fight the Doubt-Minotaur to manage it). You will hit do artist block. You will run out of steam. You will have days where every single pencil scratch looks like a 2 year old did it -

(One Last Time) The Two Most Important Words for Artists:

Courage doesn't always roar. Sometimes courage is the quiet voice at the end of the day saying 'I will try again tomorrow.'
—*Mary Anne Radmacher*

Fall seven times and stand up eight.
—*Japanese Proverb*

Have you ever felt like quitting as an artist? Well, welcome to the club…for even Michelangelo, and Da Vinci down to Disney and Marvel artists felt like there work was worthless, so drawing is worth the struggle. You can do this.. **……DON'T QUIT.**

REMEMBER ONE OTHER WORD OF ADVICE THAT HAS BEEN SAID FOR CENTURIES AND OVER AND OVER…

Heres an assaignment even if you don't want to do it…

TAKE FIFTEEN MINUTES

And go toe-to-toe with the last drawing project you either quit or wanted to quit.

And forget if there was someone doubting you?

Or thought your work was all off, or it was a bigger project than you thought?

Whatever the reason was, do the art and take the vow right now

"I WON'T QUIT!"
"I CAN DO THIS!"

DON'T FORGET TO LEAVE ENCOURAGEMENT FOR OTHER ARISTS!

NOTES

CPSIA information can be obtained
at www.ICGtesting.com
Printed in the USA
JSHW010144070321
12299JS00008B/49